THE STORY OF THE WRITINGS

BY JOSEPH ROSNER

edited by EUGENE B. BOROWITZ

illustrations by STEPHEN KRAFT

BEHRMAN HOUSE, INC.   New York

THE

STORY

OF THE

WRITINGS

Dedicated

to my niece

Laura

Published by Behrman House, Inc.

1261 Broadway, New York, N. Y.

Library of Congress Catalog Card Number: 78-116680

Standard Book Number: 87441-038-X

MANUFACTURED IN THE UNITED STATES OF AMERICA

CONTENTS

PROLOGUE

THE PART OF the Bible about which you will read here is known as the "Wisdom Literature," or the "WRITINGS." It is a detailed guide-book for helping you through the experiences that make up your lifetime. Like a road-map, it can keep you on a sensible course in your relations with others and, more importantly, with yourself. It speaks directly and personally to "you."

Questions for yesterday and today

The most recent of these WRITINGS is well over two thousand years old. You may ask: What can ideas that are so old say to me, across the gulf of all that time? The answer is simple: The physical conditions of the good life are always newer or different, but the moral ones remain always the same. You can now travel between New York and California by plane instead of covered wagon, but the values by which you travel the road of life are unchanged. The most troubling questions we ask ourselves are the same now as they were many centuries ago. For instance:

The hustler and the "operator" seem to abound and even prosper, so why should I bother to be good? Corruption is everywhere, so what is the point in my being honest? Many of my friends go all-out for pleasure, so why should I be old-fashioned? Does it really pay to study, to work, to make sacrifices for tomorrow? If I choose to "make out" above all else, what price will I pay?

These are only a few of the questions one might ask. And you will find these answered with a richness of experience that has given direction to countless generations of men, Gentile as well as Jew. The wise men who put together the WRITINGS could not tell you how to fix a flat or meet a payroll. But one can learn those techniques easily enough. The greatest problems you will face are those that affect your relations with your times, with people rather than with things. And of all your relationships, the most important by far is the one you have with yourself. Dealing with such problems is what wisdom (and this book) is all about.

What to do? What to say?

To be alive is to be forced to choose. This has never been more true than it is today. The need to make decisions is almost oppressive, and judgment is demanded of us regularly. Should I do this? Dare I refuse to do that? And what price will I pay for doing or not doing either of these? Can I get away with this? Can I ignore that? Will I hate myself in the morning, and how long will that morning last? Sometimes the choice is very serious and sometimes it is less so, but in any case it must be made. The way in which we make our choices, our judgments, usually results from how we feel about ourselves and our world.

The facts about which you will read here are rooted not only in faith but also in reason. They are indispensable to your living the best possible life *for you.* They make up a kind of Thinker's Digest of human experience, and it is just as useful today as it was thousands of years ago. No Columbus of the mind has discovered anything to cause us to change the map you will find here. It will serve as well tomorrow morning as when first set down. Moreover, it talks to you in language of unparalleled power and beauty.

Cuneiform clay tablet

The ways of wisdom

Wisdom, always and everywhere, points the way for each of us to be a man. Because a sound idea does not bow to time, or nationality, or religion, much of the world's good sense is widely shared. You will therefore notice that some of the ideas you read here will seem familiar. But in no other single work are you likely to find so much that is so worthwhile so memorably presented.

We have tried in a number of ways to make your study of the WRITINGS more pleasant. Our translation is not only in the modern style, but free enough to let the ideas come through clearly. You will find here the Hebrew of many of the most famous verses, and special quotation marks « » indicate passages you should want to know by heart. The books are not presented in the Bible's order (which varies in the older versions). They are arranged here in a

THE STORY OF THE WRITINGS

sequence that will make them, we think, more immediately interesting, understandable and useful.

When you think of the people you know and hear about, or read or hear the latest news, you may become discouraged. There seems to be such a great distance between what is and what ought to be. True. But no more or less true today than at any other time in history. Man's ideals have always raced far ahead of his behavior. To the extent that you fall behind in your own pursuit of what is ideal for you, you will suffer. This is not the verdict of the Bible alone, but of wise men everywhere.

The Wisdom Literature can point you to the way in which the good life can be pursued. But it cannot move you along the path it suggests. In that, each of us must be his own self-starter and must provide his own fuel.

PROVERBS

THE BOOK OF COMMON SENSE

CHAPTER I

GEORGE BERNARD SHAW once wrote: "Few people bother to think more than two or three times a year. But look at me—I have made an international reputation for myself just by thinking once or twice a week." Why did he write this? Because he knew that common sense is probably the most underrated commodity in the world. All of us acknowledge that it is a good thing to have. But it isn't the kind of thing everyone dreams of someday achieving. Unlike success, wealth, or being much respected, it lacks glamor. Maybe it's because of that word "common." The word throws us off, making it appear that this kind of knowledge is widespread—all over the place and easily achieved. Try a little experiment: Ask a few of your friends, separately, whether in their judgment they have common sense. None is likely to deny it.

But as Shaw well knew, common sense is *not* common. In fact, it is comparatively rare. Think of all the people you know. Pick out from among them, in your mind, those who seem to act always with good judgment, who show a sound, practical sense of the world. These people, you will soon notice, are very much in the minority. Most persons do not seem to think often enough. And they tend to make decisions as if civilization had learned nothing since it began.

It is not too harsh to say that most people make important judgments by the whims and desires and emotions of the moment. This is common *non-sense*. There is evidence of it all around us. Read history or today's newspaper: Even the men who are paid to think for us do not always do such a grand job. Bertrand Russell, the British philosopher, wrote that "the brain is that organ with which we think that we think."

As with the weather, everyone talks about common sense, but not many seem to be doing anything about it. The BOOK OF PROVERBS was put together to help you and me become uncommonly sensible.

The Jewish people have always had a special respect for wisdom and learning. This book is a wealth of such wisdom and learning. It is based on the observation and experience of various wise men of Israel over a period of a thousand years. Part of it is as down-to-earth as advice from an older brother, and part is quite spiritual in tone. It has something intelligent to say about almost every kind of situation or idea that is likely to make you wonder, *What do I do now?*

A proverb, we know, is a saying that tells a useful truth in short but expressive language. But over the centuries, proverbs have come to have a bad reputation. Many have been around for so long that we now think of them as platitudes, clichés, commonplace remarks. "Early to bed and early to rise . . ." is a bore. Such statements are victims of our tendency to be attracted to what is new. It isn't easy to get excited about something that has been lying around in history's attic for thousands of years. It doesn't seem to matter that the proverb has lasted that long because it has proved to be true. It suffers the fate of an old uncle who has always lived with us. We take him for granted. Only after he helps us through a terrible crisis do we realize what a sensible fellow the old man happens to be.

If getting old means becoming wise in what is important and what is not, then the BOOK OF PROVERBS has that kind of age. In this anthology, you will find, the Jews have distilled their practical experience from their earliest times until about their return from exile in Babylon (late Sixth Century B.C.E.). Much of this collection is in the form of very brief statements. Other parts are longer; they are poems in which we are given an extended, more rounded view of the specific idea being presented to us. And throughout these pages we are struck, over and over again, with the feeling that the men who put these words together knew a great deal about the psychology we call "modern."

Cutting reed to make pen

The first nine chapters of this book make up a kind of prologue in praise of wisdom. Wisdom is the pivot of the universe, the only sound axis on which a life may turn: "The Lord made me as the beginning of His way." Without it, we lose the good that life   *8:22* offers; with it, we gain the best that life knows. The book is typically direct in its opening lines. It tells us exactly what it seeks to do for us:

"The proverbs of Solomon . . .
That men may gain wisdom and instruction;
May understand words of intelligence;
That they may receive instruction in wise conduct,
In rectitude, justice and honesty;
That sense may be imparted to the simple,
Knowledge and discretion to the inexperienced;
The wise man also may hear and increase his learning,
The man of intelligence acquire sound principles . . ."   *1:1-5*

Notice that this does not claim to be a help only to those of us who are not particularly bright. Even the wise men can still gain in wisdom—and some of the wisest of men have been among the first to admit this. A man who thinks he knows everything he ought to know is obviously a fool.

Throughout the ages, most of the world has agreed, "Knowledge is power." But most of the world has done very little to gain such knowledge:

"If you but turn and pay heed to my admonition,
Lo! I will open my mind to you,
I will acquaint you with my thoughts.
But I called and you refused to listen,
I stretched out my hand and no one paid heed;
You ignored all my counsel,
And would not have my admonition;
So I in turn will laugh in the hour of your doom,
I will mock when your terror comes . . ."   *1:23-26*

Two things need to be said here about Hebrew poetry which will apply to everything we study. First, its main feature is not rhyme ("Jack and Jill . . . up the hill") but parallelism: The same thing is said twice or even three times, in a different way. Second, Biblical poetry almost always makes its point by what we would call "exaggeration": The poets appear to say extreme things, perhaps in the hope that by being intense they are more likely to break through to us. Now, take another look at the previous verses.

The idea here seems logical enough. You ignore good sense at your own risk. When the inevitable happens, and you look foolish because of some thoughtless act, you will remember what you should have done, and it will be too late,

> "For the waywardness of the simple shall slay them,
> And the complacency of fools shall destroy them;
> While he who listens to me shall live in security

1:32-33   And shall enjoy peace of mind without dread of evil."

Every society has a low opinion of the man who ignores the wisdom of those who have already lived through the experiences he has yet to face. A nation must understand history, to keep from repeating old mistakes. In the same way, the individual must understand experience, to keep from making other people's mistakes. Here is an Arab formula of about a thousand years ago:

> He who knows not and knows not he knows not, he is a fool—shun him!
> He who knows not and knows he knows not, he is simple—teach him;
> He who knows and knows not he knows, he is asleep—wake him;
> He who knows and knows he knows, he is wise—follow him!

The salute to reason continues with a statement of its usefulness:

> "For when wisdom finds a welcome within you,
> And knowledge becomes a pleasure to you,
> Discretion will watch over you,
> Reason will guard you—
> Saving you from the way of evil men,
> From men who use perverse speech,
> Who are crooked in their ways,

2:10-15   And tortuous in their paths . . ."

What about those very clever fellows, the "hustlers," "operators," and "con men" with whom the world seems to abound?

> "For they sleep not unless they have done mischief to someone,
> Their slumber is broken unless they have caused someone to stumble;
> The bread they eat is won by crime,

And the wine they drink is won by lawlessness.
The way of the wicked is dark as pitch;
They know not at what they stumble.
But the path of the righteous is like the light of the dawn,
That shines ever more brightly till the day is full."   *4:16-19*

This seems like wishful thinking—the way we would want things
to be. Often enough, we know, they're not that way at all. Still,
when you come to think about it, though there are exceptions, this
remains a good—if exaggerated—poetic statement of the truth.

One famous bit of wisdom emphasizes the importance of work:

"Go to the ant, O sluggard,
Study her ways, and learn wisdom;
For though she has no chief,
No officer, or ruler,
She prepares her food in the summer,
She gathers in her provisions in the fall,
How long will you rest, O sluggard?
When will you rise from your sleep?
'A little sleep, a little slumber,
A little folding of hands to rest'—
So will poverty come upon you like a bandit,
And want like an armed man."   *6:6-11*

Benjamin Franklin said much the same thing with, "Laziness
travels so slowly that poverty soon overtakes him."

In this same chapter, we get a neat listing of a number of things
this world could do without:

«Six things the Lord hates,
Seven are an abomination to Him:
Haughty eyes, a lying tongue,
And hands that shed innocent blood;
A mind that plots mischievous schemes,
Feet that are quick to run after evil;
A false witness who utters lies,
And he who sows discord among brothers.»   *6:16-19*

The last item seems to be a climax. We not only do evil, then, but
we create more evildoers.

« » These special quotation marks, you recall, enclose passages recommended
for memorizing. You may wish to memorize others of your own choosing as
well.

Keep this list in mind the next time you read a newspaper. You may be surprised to discover how easily you will be able to pin these thoughts, like labels, on some of the things you read. One reason for this is that wisdom is the common sense that is everlasting. When advice is something that works only "now," it is likely to be merely self-interest under a more respectable name.

The prologue concludes with an attack on foolishness, here personified as a shameless, vulgar woman:

> "Folly is boisterous and wanton,
> She has no sense of shame.
> She sits at the door of her house,
> On a seat by the city highways,
> Calling to all who pass by,
> Who are keeping straight on their ways;
> 'He who is simple, let him turn in here,'
> While to him who is senseless she says:
> 'Stolen water is sweet,
> And bread eaten in secret is pleasant.'
> But he knows not that the demons are there,

9:13-18 > That her guests are in the depths of Sheol."

Sheol, of course, was the underworld abode of the dead spirits.

Proverbs perhaps by Solomon

The major part of the BOOK OF PROVERBS is attributed to King Solomon. It parades before us a series of brief, common sense judgments about life and character. Many sound familiar, probably because our civilization today is supposed to be built on them. We may have actually read them, heard them, or had them handed down to us by an older person. Perhaps we have simply discovered these truths all by ourselves. But in most cases, though the language may be strange, the thought is not. It strikes home immediately with its truth. Take the opening lines:

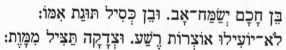

בֵּן חָכָם יְשַׂמַּח־אָב. וּבֵן כְּסִיל תּוּגַת אִמּוֹ:

לֹא־יוֹעִילוּ אוֹצְרוֹת רֶשַׁע. וּצְדָקָה תַּצִּיל מִמָּוֶת:

> "A wise son maketh a glad father;
> But a foolish son is the grief of his mother.
> Treasures born of wickedness are useless;

10:1-2 > But righteousness delivers from death."

The Sea of Bronze from Solomon's Temple

The last line has become very famous among Jews. Since the Hebrew for righteousness, *tz'dakah*, is also used in the sense of what we call "charity," this verse became a favorite for both beggars and community officials. It is often inscribed on *tz'dakah* boxes.

Every once in a while we get advice that seems, at first glance, to be almost frivolous. A closer reading makes us realize that it is actually very thoughtful:

"He who winks with the eye makes trouble;
He who reproves frankly makes peace." 10:10

That first line has nothing to do with flirting. It concerns the attitude we take to something obviously wrong or immoral. Sometimes we act as if it is nothing, harmless. As a result—silence gives consent—it is likely to get worse. To face it down immediately, to say openly that it is evil, is to keep it from doing eventual harm. Perhaps the author of these lines didn't have in mind anything quite so ambitious, but the folly of appeasing any form of tyranny is contained in this thought. The good people who winked at Hitler lived to regret it. Those who wink at crime often live to regret that, too.

Have you ever thought it fun to break the rules and get away with it?

"To a fool doing evil is like a sport,
But so is wisdom to a man of sense." 10:23

When one man drives through a red light it may not mean very much. But think what our world would be like if everybody started to do it. And if that is true with something simple, like traffic arrangements, then what would happen if we played games with our obligations to other people?

"Wealth is of no avail on the day of wrath;
But righteousness saves from death." 11:4

We have heard part of this before, and the whole statement seems to be saying something merely "pious." But think about it for a moment and you see that it takes in far more range than that. It is talking about the basic elements in living, especially when an experience is crucial to us. We are being told that there are big, harsh moments in our lives and that we cannot buy our way out of them with money. At such times it is mostly the way we feel about ourselves—not our vanity but our sense of integrity, of real worth

—that can make the difference. A doctor sees examples of this regularly. Two patients with exactly the same serious ailment may respond in completely different ways. One may suffer for a long time, even die, while another may come through almost by an effort of will. Or, to put it differently, why aren't all people who are equally rich equally happy?

Modern thinking would certainly approve the psychological basis for the following:

> "He who devotes himself to righteousness takes the road to life;
> But he who pursues wickedness is on the road to death.
>
> Those perverted in mind are an abomination to the Lord;
> But those who walk honestly are His delight.
>
> My hand upon it! the evil man will not go unpunished;
> But the race of the righteous will escape."

11:19-21

These lines are offering us a road map of sorts. On the one hand there is the path of integrity. On the other there is the path that violates every ethical standard. Will the man who takes the first path always become president of his company? No. Will he who takes the second always be struck down by a divine thunderbolt? No. But the idea is still sound. It's enough to understand that the man who really feels he is doing right is likely to be on reasonably good terms with himself, physically as well as mentally.

The man who makes a practice of violating society's agreed-upon rules is in for trouble. Going against the rest of us is hard work, with physical as well as emotional effects. Only a man without a conscience will be unaffected. There are such people, and they often mislead us with their charm, but because they have no real sense of right and wrong they are hardly human. Most people aren't that bad. But they often live in such a way as to suffocate their conscience. They may not feel the damage or show it, but they are, in fact, destroying the self they might have been. It has been observed that while our conscience does not always prevent us from committing a sin, it usually prevents us from enjoying it.

Here is an ancient definition of a "phony":

> "Better a man of low rank, who works for himself,
> Than he who assumes honor, yet has nothing to eat."

12:9

Again,

> "One man pretends to be rich, yet has nothing;
> Another man pretends to be poor, yet has great wealth."

13:7

Many of us can think of modern examples of such men, too, that we have met or heard about. But then, almost everything in this vast accumulation of experience and insight has its applications for the world we know now.

Here is another comment on appearance and reality:

"Even in laughter the heart may be aching;
And the end of joy may be sorrow."

14:13

On its most obvious level, we are being told that life can be a very complex business. Joy and sorrow are not always as simple as they seem. It isn't just that people fool you; we often fool ourselves. But it is unlikely to be for long. Our foolishness must be paid for. So the wise man will be concerned with consequences as well as feelings. The verse reminds us of people who say, "I'm going to hate myself for this in the morning," but do the foolish thing anyway.

When the BOOK OF PROVERBS tells us,

"The poor man is hated even by his neighbor;
But the rich has many friends,"

14:20

it will occur to us that there are exceptions to that first line. Many wise and good men have been poor and beloved. They had no trouble being liked by those around them. Lincoln, Gandhi, and Albert Schweitzer were not amply supplied with credit cards, but many people followed and admired them. The millions of ordinary poor, however, are rarely as respected as their rich relatives. The second line of the proverb rings a loud bell. Not everybody likes a rich man, but it often seems that way. When a man is rich, people gather around him. When his spending includes others, they are anxious to enjoy his company. Ambrose Bierce, the American cynic, wrote that the word "acquaintance" could be defined as "a degree of friendship called slight when its object is poor and obscure, and intimate when he is rich and famous."

Assyrian king in chariot

Every doctor knows that peace of mind provides a defense against illness. The mind in a state of unrest will leave the body prey to all kinds of ailments. This is the central idea of psychosomatic medicine. The Hebrew wise men put it this way:

"A tranquil mind is health for the body;
But passion is a rot in the bones. . . .

14:30

"A glad heart makes a bright face;
But through sadness of heart the spirit is broken. . . .

15:13

19

"For the miserable man every day is unhappy;
But the cheerful man enjoys a perpetual feast.
Better a little, with reverence for the Lord,

15:15-16   Than much treasure, and anxiety with it."

If you feel bad, then everything in your life will be discolored by the misery you feel, and vice versa. And going further, life can be much more pleasant with modest means if you believe in what is true and lasting than with great riches plus a belief in the value of wealth alone. If money was all that counted, rich people would never have nervous breakdowns or commit suicide. Mind you, there are no proverbs that tell us we will be happier if we are poorer, or that we should not try to make money. All they say, and they say it again and again, is that money is not God. Money is very useful, but it is very far from being the most important thing to us.

Everywhere in these pages the authors are in favor of life, cheer, the good heart. Life is a serious business, they seem to be telling us, but it should not be taken too seriously. Don't be too solemn about it. You can lead the good life and enjoy it, and it's even healthier that way.

And what about those times when we may do wrong? Do we usually hurry to admit the error of our ways? This is hardly likely:

"All the ways of a man are pure in his own eyes;

16:2   But the Lord weighs the motives."

You should be able to think, without too much trouble, of some time when you were wrong and yet tried to put the best possible face on your error. You explained. You used just the right emphasis and left out only a few of the facts. You did a fine job of plastic surgery on what you had done. But in your heart you knew you were wrong. People do this kind of thing, businesses do it, and governments do it, too. With you and me, it's called "rationalization." With a business, it's called "public relations." A government calls it "diplomacy." But being clever doesn't change the sin. Here it makes things worse, because it keeps us from putting things right.

Life is a testing ground for each of us, and time and again the PROVERBS make that point. Here are some lines that remind us of the trials of Job:

"Like the smelter for silver, and the furnace for gold,
    The Lord is a tester of hearts." 17:3

As any sensible person knows, there are always situations in which
"the men are separated from the boys." Only toughness of spirit,
faith in what we are about, will see us through such an ordeal with
success.

A roll call of reason

One after another, an army of insights about life and people
marches before us.

"A rebuke sinks deeper into a man of intelligence
    Than a hundred lashes into a fool." 17:10

Injustice?

"He who acquits the guilty, and he who condemns
        the innocent—
    Both of them are an abomination to the Lord." 17:15

Deviousness?

"He who is perverse in mind will meet with no good;
    And he who is crooked in speech will fall into trouble." 17:20

Friends and others?

«There are friends who play at friendship;
    And there is a friend who sticks closer than a brother.» 18:24

Luck, fate, and the influence of the stars?

"A man's folly ruins his business;
    Then he rages against the Lord." 19:3

The embarrassment of poverty?

"A poor man's brothers all hate him;
    How much more do his friends stand aloof from him!
    When he pursues them with words,
    They are gone." 19:7

Your conscience, the toughest judge of all?

"Bread won by fraud tastes sweet to a man;
    But afterward his mouth will be filled with gravel." 20:17

Honest business dealings?
> "Diverse weights are an abomination to the Lord;
20:23   And false scales are not good."

Fake charity?
> "Sacrifice from wicked men is an abomination;
21:27   The more so when they offer it as an atonement for crime."

Economic injustice?
> "The rich rules over the poor;
22:7   And the borrower is a slave to the lender."

Personal honor?

נִבְחָר שֵׁם מֵעשֶׁר רָב. מִכֶּסֶף וּמִזָּהָב חֵן טוֹב:

> "A good name is rather to be chosen than great riches,
22:1   And loving favor rather than silver and gold."

Compare this last one with what Shakespeare wrote, some two thousand years later, in *Othello:*
> "Good name in man and woman . . .
> Is the immediate jewel of their souls.
> Who steals my purse steals trash . . .
> But he that filches from me my good name
> Robs me of that which not enriches him
> And makes me poor indeed."

Should you fraternize with fanatics of any kind?
> "Form no friendship with a hot-tempered man,
> And with a passionate man go not;
> Lest you learn his ways,
22:24-25   And get yourself into a snare."

Honest labor?
> "You see a man skilled at his work?
> He will stand in the presence of kings;
22:29   He will not stand in the presence of obscure men."

Does success mean making a lot of money?
> "Toil not to become rich,
23:4   Seek not superfluous wealth!"

In fact, take another look at 22:1 above to refresh your memory about something superior to money. And another reading of 16:16 will indicate other virtues far superior to riches.

Occasionally, as we have noticed earlier, there are observations which are less brief and direct. At such times the lines roll out poetically. They are shot through with dramatic images, usually meant to persuade us of an especially important point. Here, for example, is one of the most stirring editorials ever written against the perils of alcohol. Many of its phrases will seem familiar. They should. They have become part of the world's vocabulary. Across the centuries, whenever drunkenness has been condemned, these lines have provided much of the basic ammunition. The Prohibition movement in America used these words regularly. Jews have never been Prohibitionists, but they have always had an unusually low number of alcoholics. The wisdom of these words became the life practice of our people:

Ancient wine cup

"Who have woe? Who have pain?
Who have strife? Who have complaints?
Who have wounds without cause?
Who have redness of eyes?
Those who stay long over wine,
Who go often to test the mixture!
Look not on wine when it is red,
When it sparkles in the cup.
It may go down smoothly;
But at the end it bites like a serpent,
And stings like an adder.
You will see strange sights,
And will utter weird words;
You will be like a man asleep at sea,
Asleep in the midst of a violent storm.
'They may strike me, but I feel no pain;
They may beat me, but I know it not.
When shall I awake from my wine,
That I may seek it again?' "

23:29-35

In a very direct sense, this passage is telling us not to become enslaved by alcohol. Less directly, it warns against being enslaved by *anything* that will cause us to sweep reason under some carpet of the mind. To drink too much is one way to reduce yourself to the level of a non-being, someone whose intelligence can no longer control his actions. But there are other indulgences that may cause this to happen. Abusing the mind with drugs is one of these. There are more. The BOOK OF PROVERBS hoists a warning flag over all of them.

More than once, the BOOK OF PROVERBS appears to have a political tone that is conservative to the point of being unethical. This may reflect the fact that for many periods of their history the Jews were the subjects of powerful alien rulers. To rebel at such times might simply have meant immediate repression and bloodshed. So:

"My son, reverence the Lord and the king,
And meddle not with those of high rank;
For suddenly ruin will come at their hands,
And who knows the doom that both of them can bring?"

24:21-22

Respect power and don't fight it, this seems to say. Keep cool. There are times when that is certainly wise, as in the face of the total power and authority that characterized earlier tyrannies. But in our own era, a policy like that could lead to an apathy or appeasement that could perpetuate evil. In a democracy, particularly, not to get involved can be a great failing.

But it is often not easy to know when to fight and when to accept the way things are. We get some help in a famous pair of lines:

"The wicked flee when no man pursues;
But the righteous are as bold as a lion."

28:1

That first line warns that when you feel guilty about something, nervous, anxious and unsure, you will see phantoms everywhere. Every touch and shadow, every knock on the door or sound at the window, every auto horn from far away will make you jump. Your own fear will make you see the prospect of exposure and punishment in almost everything that surrounds you. You'll be afraid to challenge anybody. In contrast, when you feel sure that you are doing the right thing, it encourages a sense of fearlessness toward the world through which you move. And it helps in facing new situations to know that in previous cases you have found a way to do the good more often than not. But that goal is not always so easy to achieve, for,

"There is a class of people who curse their father,
And do not bless their mother.
There is a class of people who are pure in their own eyes,
Yet are not cleansed of their filthiness.
There is a class of people with oh! such haughty eyes,
And such uplifted eyelids.
There is a class of people whose teeth are swords,
And whose fangs are knives,
To devour the poor from the earth,
And the needy from among men."   *30:11-14*

It shouldn't be hard to think of people who fit into one or more
details of this general picture.

A smile can often make things much easier to bear. If we read
with care, we can detect a glint of mockery or humor in this comment:

"Under three things the earth quakes,
Under four it cannot bear up:
A slave when he becomes a king,
A fool when he is sated with food,
An unpopular woman when she is married,
And a maidservant when she supplants her mistress."   *30:21-23*

In a chapter attributed to "King Lemuel," we are given a capsule
version of the Hebrew ethic as it applies to social justice:

«Open your mouth on behalf of the dumb,
In defense of the rights of all who are suffering;
Open your mouth on the side of justice,
And defend the rights of the poor and the needy.»   *31:8-9*

In praise of the good wife

Throughout this commentary on human experience, the BOOK
OF PROVERBS has things to say about women, many quite unflatter-
ing. For instance:

"A foolish son is his father's ruin;
And a quarrelsome wife is like water continually dripping."   *19:13*

We are later advised (21:9) that even the corner of a housetop is
more pleasant to live on than a big house with "a quarrelsome
wife"; even living in a desert is better than having to put up with
such a woman (21:19). Or:

"A constant drip on a rainy day
And a quarrelsome wife are alike;
He who would restrain her would restrain the wind,

27:15-16   Or grasp oil with his right hand."

Well, what are we to say about this? There seems to be an objection here to the quarrelsome woman. But wouldn't we have similar objections to the quarrelsome man? When we read the occasional remark like this, reasonable people will think of the fact that the Bible was written by men and its wisdom was intended essentially for other men. It tempts the imagination to think what might have been included in these books had they been written exclusively by women.

But with its last words, the BOOK OF PROVERBS gives a salute to "the good wife." In twenty-two separate verses, the virtues of the ideal woman, wife, and mother, are celebrated for us in a way not found in most other religious literature. Here are the opening and closing lines of the poem:

אֵשֶׁת־חַיִל מִי יִמְצָא. וְרָחֹק מִפְּנִינִים מִכְרָהּ:

"If one can find a good wife,
She is worth far more than corals.
Her husband puts his trust in her,
And finds no lack of gain.
She brings him good, and not harm,

31:10-12   All the days of his life. . . .

"Her children rise up, and bless her—
Her husband also, and praises her:
'Many women have done well,
But you have excelled them all.'
Charm is deceptive, and beauty is a breath;
But a woman who reveres the Lord—she will be praised.
Give her the due reward of her work;

31:28-31   And let her deeds bring her praise at the gates."

Students of civilization have noted that you can usually tell how advanced a culture is just by the respect it accords to its women. The Hebrew culture was the first to take woman out of the class of household possessions, a kind of superior domestic animal, and set her distinction down in words.

Did Solomon write all these proverbs, as that very first line tells us? Highly unlikely. For one thing, parts of the text, later, profess to be from "Agur the son of Jakeh," and from "Lemuel," the king $30:1$ of Massa. For another thing, this book speaks out fairly often about $31:1$ kings, but not always as if they were invariably wise and just. That sounds more like the wisdom of common men than kings.

Another point we might consider is the tone of this book. Unlike other parts of the Bible, this one concentrates less on the Hebrew nation and more on the individual, the man and woman who are Jews. This concern, some scholars feel, developed after the return from Babylon. And this, of course, would place the book long after the time of Solomon. But that is pure speculation. We simply do not know. It seems reasonable to believe, however, that some of the material here originated with him. Traditionally, his wisdom was an ornament of Judaism, and there are many things in the book which even an early wise man could well have known.

In this work, every reader will notice that he is being addressed personally. *You* are the target. The writings are aimed directly at the reader, who is considered to be worth all this attention. The average man, it is assumed here, is wise enough to want to become wiser.

The tone of this book is quite different from that of the TORAH or the PROPHETS. Nothing written here is imposed on anyone as an order or a commandment. The men who wrote PROVERBS did not represent themselves as delegates from God. The only authority they depend on is that of superior experience, learning, and "common sense."

But good sense alone is not enough. These ideas also take it for granted that virtue is an indispensable element in a man's life. The authors of these words felt that any line of conduct which runs against the sense of what they offer here as wisdom was wrong. But why? Because it was bound to be unrealistic, or antisocial, or self-destructive, or even criminal. It could not last. It was doomed to failure in one way or another.

We find here the heart of the Jewish tradition that to lead the good life, the life of wisdom and virtue, will bring happiness, while sin will bring the reverse. It is an extension of the idea that God

Pre-exilic Israelite

is just. It claims that the universe moves most smoothly through space and time when its guiding principles are right and good. Are there occasional contradictions to this belief that goodness brings happiness and sin brings misery? Of course. Such contradictions raise questions that have always troubled men of good will. The BOOK OF JOB attempts to answer these questions.

Unlike JOB or even ECCLESIASTES, there is no sense of deep thinking or philosophy in this book. The authors present everything to us ready-made, neatly packaged. We are given the stripped-down findings of many centuries of observation and experience. Pithy and concrete, they seem to leave little room for changing one's position or thought in the face of new situations or needs. But they served in their time—and still serve—a great purpose for the average man. Like a compass bearing, they gave him a sense of direction, a sense of the right course, through the turmoil we call "history." They helped him to a feeling of unity with his fellows, to a feeling of his own power in the world. And they gave him something that each of us needs, a capacity for enthusiasm in the living of a good and worthy life.

What we believe and what we do

If you follow every bit of advice in this book, are you sure to be a howling success at everything you attempt? No. Life has too many surprises for anyone, no matter how wise he may be. None of us can hope to get through life without occasional shock, loss, or even disaster. But a firm grasp of what this book has to offer would give you an understanding of what is *right* as well as useful to know. And if the unforeseen *should* strike, you are likely to be better prepared for it. In that part of your life which you have still to live—it begins a moment from now—there are many situations which are unknowns. The more good sense you bring into your encounters with those situations, the more likely you are to succeed in them.

Good sense is not a gift. Nor can you become wise just by committing all these sayings to memory. It might help you to think of wisdom as a muscle. If it is not used, it will become atrophied, like any other unused muscle. Then it is useless. Perhaps you know someone of whom this is true, someone who seems smart but acts foolish. Such a person is likely to make us feel sad. In your own case, if you wish this muscle to work for you, then you must use it over and over. It becomes better with exercise and develops through experience. Wisdom, of course, is not actually a muscle. Nor is character. But what we are really talking about is the *building* of character.

Wisdom is a good thing for any man to have, but it is not quite enough. There are situations in which even the wisest of us are beyond our resources. A death in the family, serious illness, a great natural catastrophe. . . . At such times we may require something that goes beyond the limits of our own capacity for wisdom. It is then that we gather strength from something that transcends what is normally comprehensible. We call that "faith," and from that faith we receive the energy to endure, to go on.

The men who wrote these proverbs knew that wisdom could not do it all. The Prophets, elsewhere in the Bible, knew that, too. They preached the values of faith and righteousness, because they knew that man's real struggles often take place outside himself, beyond those things he can see, hear, and touch. In that realm there are no real facts. But that is where belief is born, the belief that there is wisdom, that wisdom is good, and that man can live by it. And at bottom is the belief that this wisdom comes from God Himself.

ESTHER

THE IMPORTANCE OF UNITY

CHAPTER 2

THE AVERAGE football team has eleven men. But suppose you were walking onto the field for a game in which your own team had only three men, including yourself? And you knew that the game was "legal," and that it would probably last a lifetime? Very tough, of course. Yet that has been the position of almost every minority throughout history. It has usually had to face a majority that could ordinarily overwhelm it not only with superior numbers, but with the power of the law.

When someone has an appearance (or holds to ideas) which are "different," he is often headed for trouble. So it was with the American colonist who thought he ought to be free of England. So it has been with the Negro in this country and elsewhere. It is true as well of today's student activist. And through most of modern history it has been especially true of the Jew. He has been vastly outnumbered in the game of life. For this reason, teamwork has been essential in the way he played the game. More than most men, he has had to learn to make decisions quickly and to act upon them. You may recall in your own life an experience in which the odds were against you, but you came through by acting with decision.

Every nation has stories which may not be entirely true, but which serve a useful purpose. In each case they teach us a lesson of some kind. Aesop's fables are like that. So is the story of George Washington chopping down that cherry tree. The BOOK OF ESTHER is another. It is longer and more interesting than most, and far richer in detail, but very probably it is not true—that is, it probably never happened. There are too many obvious exaggerations. There are things in it that do not square with what we know from other, more reliable, historical sources.

But this story has one thing in common with other famous ones. The separate and even false details are less important than something that they all add up to: one great truth. In this case, the truth is the Jewish sense of community, the need for all Jews to stand together as one.

Any minority, when its members lock arms to act as one, will always have a far greater chance to make its strength felt. When Benjamin Franklin signed the Declaration of Independence, he said, "We must all hang together, or assuredly we will all hang separately." Even when a man is actually alone, his own sense of rightness in what he is about will add fuel to his cause. The Texas Rangers have a motto that goes something like this: "A little man can always take a big man, if he just keeps coming." And the Jews have always been, wherever they have been in the world, "a little man."

The story of ESTHER takes place in a distant country and in a distant time, but its outlines are as familiar as many of the films we see on television or at the movies. There is a villain who falls into his own trap, and there are good people who conquer their enemies and then live happily ever after. With minor changes here and there, ESTHER is really a classic romance which tells of the triumph of good over evil. Briefly, here is what happens:

A great king of Persia, Ahasuerus, holds a banquet for his nobles that lasts for six months. (It is hard to know whether to admire or to feel sorry for anyone who knows how to make a dinner last that long.) The king follows this immediately with a more modest party that lasts for only one week. On the seventh day of this more casual celebration, while "joyous with wine," he demands that his queen, Vashti, display her beauty before his companions. She refuses. The men at the party are appalled by this refusal. They see it as a bad example for other wives in the kingdom. After all, they too might learn to disobey their husbands. The king, perhaps nervously, sends out a royal message that "every man should be master in his own house."

But this is not enough. Like a man who is dissatisfied with a secretary, the king then decides to acquire a new and more obedient

Assyrian ivory mirror

1:10

1:22

queen. He chooses a delightful method for getting one that he will be sure to like. From all over the kingdom, beautiful girls are to be brought to him, and from among them he will select a new wife. It is "Miss America," Persian style.

One of the women brought to the royal harem for this purpose is Esther. She is an orphan who has been raised in the house of Mordecai, her cousin. The king is not aware that she is Jewish, and in time he selects her as his queen. He makes a great feast to celebrate this event, and as far as we know, the new queen presents the king with no special problems there. They are very happy together.

Meanwhile, back in the city, Mordecai is able to be of additional service to the king. He hears of a plot to assassinate the ruler, and passes the information to Esther. She warns her husband, and the plot is foiled.

During this period, a man named Haman becomes the king's prime minister. Because Mordecai will not bow down before him, as royal decree ordains, Haman becomes furious not only at Mordecai, but every member of his faith. It is something like the episode of Vashti. Here again someone from a "subordinate" class refuses to act as expected, and a sort of panic follows. Haman decides on a revenge, however, that the history of our own time has made familiar. He will not only hang Mordecai, but will annihilate every Jew in the kingdom. When the Nazis, thousands of years later, tried to work out this same blueprint, they called it "the Final Solution."

To encourage the king to permit this pogrom, Haman promises a gift of 10,000 talents which someone has figured might come to more than twenty million of our dollars. This kind of thing happens even today. A government may be persuaded to do something morally wrong, or stop doing something morally right, because of the money, the territory, or the power that will accrue.

Mordecai gets word to Esther about the plan to destroy her people, informing her that she must intercede with the king. But, she points out to him, the king has not sent for her in a month. She is forbidden, on pain of death, to enter his presence until she is asked. But Mordecai convinces her that she *must* speak to the king. There are times when each of us must stick his neck out, no matter what the risk. Esther decides to try it.

The king forgives Esther for thrusting herself into his presence. She persuades him to have Haman join them at a dinner, and after a series of artful complications, the villain and his plans are overthrown. The gallows built by Haman to hang Mordecai is then used to hang Haman, instead. His fate has a kind of poetic justice, about which the Bible makes its usual sound point:

"He who digs a pit will fall into it."   *Proverbs 26:27*

To cap it all, the Jews are not only spared destruction, but are permitted to destroy their enemies. Also, many Persians become converted to the Jewish faith. As one of the more obvious results of this, the Feast of Purim is established.

The facts behind the story

In the first line of this tale, we are introduced to one of the great kings of antiquity. Here he is called Ahasuerus, but that name is unknown to us. Some scholars have identified him as Xerxes, and we know that Xerxes ruled the enormous empire of Persia from 485 until 465 B.C.E., when he died at the hands of an assassin. So much for history.

Sometimes an interesting story, even when it is true, will make us feel a bit suspicious. Do you believe everything about every story you read in the newspapers? Everything in the speech of the average politician? Every detail in the gossip about famous persons? The BOOK OF ESTHER is like some of these, only more troublesome. It is a little too perfect and it includes a number of details that are a bit hard to swallow. It rests on the marriage of a Jewish girl to the greatest king of his time, but there is no record of Xerxes having made such a marriage. Moreover, the marriages of Persian kings were strictly governed by law. Then we are told of a feast that lasted half a year. When the king was seeking a new queen, each of the *1:3-4* candidates was put through a series of beauty treatments that lasted *2:12* a full year. And we are told that the gallows built by Haman to hang Mordecai was fifty cubits high, which means that it would *5:14* have reached at least eighty feet into the air. Hanging a man from such a height would have been very spectacular, but why go to so much trouble to hang a single man? Especially when the lesson would be lost on other Jews, since they too were programmed for immediate destruction.

Scholars have other doubts about the story. They note that while the Hebrew name of this heroine of Israel was Hadassah, meaning "myrtle," the name Esther is not Hebrew at all. It is of Mesopotamian origin and very much like the name Ishtar, or Astarte, the Babylonian goddess of love. And love is one of the main ingredients in the story. In addition, the name Mordecai is similar to Marduk, and Marduk was the chief god of the people of Babylon.

Head representing Marduk

But with all its exaggerations and improbable incidents, there are areas in which the story is quite accurate. It was unmistakably written by someone who was familiar with the everyday customs and appearance of the Persian court at the time of Xerxes. The physical aspects of the palace, its official manners, the arrangements of the royal harem, all these, as set down here, are apparently correct. They are corroborated by what we read of the court in the works of Greek historians.

Some scholars think the book echoes an event which did happen in Persian times. Others think it was put in its present form more than three centuries after the time of Xerxes. The plan of Haman to exterminate the Jews appears to echo the tyranny of Antiochus Epiphanes, the Grecian ruler against whom the Maccabees revolted in 168 B.C.E. The turning of the tables, in which the destroyer is himself destroyed, thus becomes a statement of hope in the success of the Maccabees. The old Persian tale now speaks to modern times. It brings a message of hope to all Jews fighting great enemies.

Another interesting detail in the Bible story is the point about the non-Jews who became converts to Judaism. It is the only place in the Bible in which we read of such a thing. While conversion was common in the time of the Maccabean kings, and then in the era of the Rabbis, the earlier books of the Bible do not directly mention it. Some scholars see this as supporting the judgment that the book was put in its present form in the time of the Maccabees.

The meaning of the story

If any group, anywhere, is to endure in any positive way, then each member must have a feeling of community, of *belonging* to that particular group. This is a fact of all social experience. Whenever a nation's survival is in danger, its people are bombarded with slogans, songs, and stories which stress the need for unity. The message is always the same: Close ranks and join hands, the better to hold off the enemy. Once the crisis is past, the memory of the message fades. During the Arab-Israeli Six-Day War of 1967, there was unanimity among American Jews in support of the Israelis; soon, however, the enthusiasm died down. But the story of Esther is a unique rallying cry. It has lived on for centuries because the truths it tells are not only those of the moment, but for all time.

For instance: To secure permission from the king for the pogrom against them, Haman referred to the Jews in this way:

"There is a certain people scattered abroad and dispersed among the peoples throughout all the provinces of your kingdom, and their laws are different from every other people's; neither do they observe the king's laws; therefore it is not fitting to leave them alone." *3:8*

With only slight changes to serve the needs of time and place, these words have been used throughout the past. They have been the basis for persecution and discrimination, not only against the Jews, but against many other peoples whose only crime was that they appeared to be "different." The difference could be a matter of politics, or religion, or color, or almost anything else. As an obvious example, many young men and women of today, because of their unusual dress and attitudes, have become to others "a certain people" who are "different." And these others feel that "it is not fitting to leave them alone."

This story offers another passage whose meaning is as true today as it must have been many centuries ago. When Esther learns of the plot to kill the Jews, and Mordecai warns her to intercede with the king, she thinks of a reason why she should not expose herself. Mordecai's answer is well worth remembering: "Do not imagine that because you are in the royal palace you will escape any more than the other Jews. If you remain silent at this time, relief and deliverance will arise for the Jews from some other place, but you and your father's family will be destroyed; . . ." *4:13-14*

He was telling her what every Jew has had to learn throughout history. For him there is no place to hide. Under Hitler and his Nuremberg Laws, those who thought they had escaped through status, or wealth, or conversion, or changing their names or noses, or through other devices, were all, in time, rooted out and treated as "Jews." There was no escaping Jewish destiny—in this case, tragedy. And so it has usually been in our history.

Most American Jews learned from Hitler. Before World War II they had been trying to run away from being what they are. In many ways they were ashamed of it. There are Jews even today—you probably know some—who try to hide the fact that they are Jewish. But they are the minority among us now. Most American Jews have learned to be proud of their Jewishness. That doesn't mean one has to go around boasting of it; but it is certainly something one shouldn't feel ashamed of. Like Esther, there are many who seem to do little about being Jewish, but they stand with their brothers when they are needed.

There is another important point here. Esther was a queen. She was entitled to special privilege. She wasn't another, ordinary Jew. She was so far above the rest of her people that everyone thought of her as quite separate from them. Why should she, who had everything everyone else really wanted, risk her life for her people?

We see examples of this all the time. There are Jews who become rich, or powerful, or famous, who like to forget they are Jews. They do not want to help their people. To prove that they have no special ties to their heritage, they may even go to the extreme of discriminating against whatever reminds them of it. This has perhaps been especially noticeable—and dangerous—in America, where there is such great opportunity to advance to positions of eminence. The BOOK OF ESTHER is more than an example of just what any decent person should do when his people is in trouble. Do *everything* you can, it says. Don't turn your back on your own. Through the words of Mordecai it makes the additional realistic point that no Jew is so powerful that he can ever really hide.

Purim

There is nothing like the downfall of an enemy to serve as a reason for celebration. Almost every nation has a holiday that celebrates its freedom from some kind of oppression. After the defeat of Haman, Mordecai went out to his people dressed like a king. And

לַיְּהוּדִים הָיְתָה אוֹרָה וְשִׂמְחָה וְשָׂשֹׂן וִיקָר:

8:16 «The Jews had light and gladness and joy and honor.»

These words are still used in the *Havdalah* ritual at the end of the Sabbath, as a classic description of Jewish joy. Then Mordecai sent letters to all his people, telling them to commemorate their victory,

כַּיָּמִים אֲשֶׁר־נָחוּ בָהֶם הַיְּהוּדִים מֵאוֹיְבֵיהֶם. וְהַחֹדֶשׁ אֲשֶׁר
נֶהְפַּךְ לָהֶם מִיָּגוֹן לְשִׂמְחָה וּמֵאֵבֶל לְיוֹם טוֹב. לַעֲשׂוֹת אוֹתָם
יְמֵי מִשְׁתֶּה וְשִׂמְחָה. וּמִשְׁלוֹחַ מָנוֹת אִישׁ לְרֵעֵהוּ וּמַתָּנוֹת
לָאֶבְיֹנִים׃

"the days wherein the Jews had rest from their enemies, and the
month which was turned unto them from sorrow to gladness . . .
and of sending portions one to another, and gifts to the poor." *9:22*

The holiday gets its name from the fortunetelling routine by
which Haman chose the day of destruction. There was a casting of
lots, or Purim, so that the chosen day would be exactly right, according to local superstition. The date selected, in the month of
Adar, turned out to be, instead, the occasion for Haman's death.
It is that date on which the holiday is now celebrated.

Purim is a feast of joy, of jokes and noisemaking. As such, it
makes a welcome change from the solemnity of most Jewish holy
days. In medieval times, in fact, celebration was given a very free
hand. It could be carried on till the drinker of wine could no longer
tell the difference between "Blessed is Mordecai" and "Cursed is
Haman." And even now, when a powerful man tries to visit hatred
and destruction on the Jews, he is invariably called a Haman.

Outside the BOOK OF ESTHER, the Bible gives no hint of the
origins of the Feast of Purim. Scholars have suggested that it may
have been, originally, a national festival of Persia, celebrated by
the Jews during their captivity in that kingdom. Later, these scholars
believe, it was brought to life again, at a time when the Jewish
people were in the throes of a political revival under the Maccabean
kings. The story was perhaps written then to promote in Jerusalem
a day that had been celebrated with joy during an unhappier time.

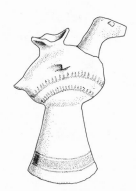

Mesopotamian jug

The BOOK OF ESTHER is the only book in the Bible that does
not mention God. The Jews, in their crisis, are able to save themselves without the direct intervention of the Lord. In this way, the
story gives us another important point about life: Until a good
miracle comes along, it is always wise to get on with the job
yourself.

But Jewish tradition had learned from the rest of the Bible
an equally important point: Man's work, when it is against God's
will, is futile. Man is most successful when he and God are partners.

RUTH

THE WOMAN NOT LIKE OTHERS

CHAPTER 3

THE STORY OF RUTH, the woman of Moab, is not a dramatic one. There are no battles in it, no villains, and no struggles for power. The characters are farmers, and nothing that happens to them is meant to be very exciting. That is the way life is for most of us. And yet this story is one of the best known in the Bible. The reason may be that it is so beautifully written. Some, in fact, have called it the first great short story. Then again, the reason may be that the values with which it deals—tolerance and loyalty—have never elsewhere been dealt with quite so well.

At any given time in history, the world has had a plentiful supply of outsiders, and for them this quiet tale has always been timely. We live now in a period we choose to call modern, nearly three thousand years after these events might have happened. Yet the story of Ruth speaks to us. It is as topical as conformity, "doing your own thing," and that old standby, love.

Like Esther among the Persians, Ruth was different. Almost every culture has a way of drawing a line around certain groups of people. So do families and groups of friends. Some people are "in." Some are "out." These lines that people draw usually carry a warning, in invisible letters: Do Not Cross. Custom and experience tell us what is not visible to the eye. Nor is it easy to violate such a line, to make a friend on the other side of it. Try to cross a line that divides social classes, or even one that separates cliques within a class, and you may pay a heavy price for that new friendship.

One of the bigger problems in the world is the ease with which many people find a way to feel superior to others. Politics, color, and religion are only some of the more obvious ways. Think of these:

I have more money than you.
I am older than you.
I am under thirty and you can't understand me.
I am male and you are only female.
I live here and you are a stranger.
I eat meat and you are a vegetarian.
I am hip and you are square.

Wherever differences exist, there are those who will seize on them to keep people apart. People will exploit the most trivial things to create such conflict. Lines are drawn.

The BOOK OF RUTH is about the crossing of lines, lines of folk, of religion, of age. It tells us all that anyone has to know about loyalty and tolerance, about conscience and courage.

They are related themes. Loyalty is the ability to stick with something or someone you believe in; tolerance is the ability to respect something or someone the other fellow believes in. Conscience helps us know what we believe, and courage enables us to live it, despite the fads about us. Ruth shows all these qualities.

When we take a look at the past we can see that such virtues, like so many others, have usually been in short supply. And we are not oversupplied with them in the present either. The lure of the dollar, of power, of any temporary advantage, puts a strain on many loyalties and on tolerance. It can blind the conscience and smother courage.

Ask yourself: Have most people on whom you counted very much *always* proved worthy of your trust? We live in a world where special honor is supposed to be given to those who stand fast for what they believe. Of course, in many cases this honor will come to them only after they are dead. Socrates, Thoreau, and Gandhi, to name a very few, were imprisoned for their beliefs. But at our best, we respect the man who isn't always realistic, who's enough of an idealist to disturb our complacency, to prod us to become better people. Something in us admires the man who sticks all the way with a friend or an idea that he believes in.

And one of the nicer things about the BOOK OF RUTH is that

its points are made in a tranquil tone which gives additional weight to what it is saying to us. We are so accustomed to exaggeration in Biblical style, and there is so much shouting about everything today, that we may miss the message here because it is presented so gently.

The story

In the time when the judges ruled, the tale begins, a famine struck the land. Because of this, a man named Elimelech left Bethlehem with his wife and two sons, and went off to Moab. There were no Jews in this land, which was to the east of the Dead Sea. In fact, the Moabites, in later years, were among the greatest enemies of the Jews. After Elimelech had lived among these strangers for a while, he died, leaving his widow Naomi to take care of the two boys. In time, the sons, Mahlon and Chilion, married Moabite girls, Orpah and Ruth. About ten years later, both sons died.

Oxen and plow

With her sons gone, Naomi felt homesick for her own country. Besides, she had heard that conditions were much improved there. When she decided to return to her homeland, both of her daughters-in-law wished to accompany her. She felt they would do better to stay behind, among their own countrymen: "Go, return each of you to her mother's house. May the Lord deal as kindly with you as you have dealt with the dead and with me!" They ought to stay in Moab, she told them, because they would be able to find new husbands among their own people.

Orpah was convinced by this and kissed Naomi good-bye. But Ruth refused to leave. Naomi persisted: "See," she said, "your sister-in-law has turned back to her own people and her own gods; turn back after your sister-in-law."

Ruth then stated her feelings in one of the most poetic speeches to be found in the Bible:

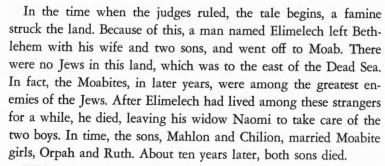

אַל־תִּפְגְּעִי־בִי לְעָזְבֵךְ לָשׁוּב מֵאַחֲרָיִךְ. כִּי אֶל־אֲשֶׁר תֵּלְכִי אֵלֵךְ וּבַאֲשֶׁר תָּלִינִי אָלִין. עַמֵּךְ עַמִּי וֵאלֹהַיִךְ אֱלֹהָי: בַּאֲשֶׁר תָּמוּתִי אָמוּת וְשָׁם אֶקָּבֵר. כֹּה יַעֲשֶׂה יְיָ לִי וְכֹה יוֹסִיף כִּי הַמָּוֶת יַפְרִיד בֵּינִי וּבֵינֵךְ:

«Entreat me not to leave thee, and to return from following after thee; for whither thou goest, I will go; and where thou lodgest, I will lodge; thy people shall be my people, and thy God my God; where thou diest, will I die, and there will I be buried. The Lord punish me, and more, if aught but death part thee and me.»

1:16-17

Orpah's loyalty to her gods was balanced here by Ruth's loyalty to Naomi. Ruth would become one of Naomi's people and worship their God. She pledged her life to it.

Convinced, Naomi permitted her to come along. They arrived together in Beth-lehem at the time of the barley harvest.

Ruth gleaning grain

A relative of Naomi's husband lived in the town, a man named Boaz, who was rather well-to-do. Ruth went off into his field to glean corn. This was the old Jewish way of caring for the poor. They could gather up for themselves what had been forgotten, dropped, or left for them. Ruth attracted the attention of Boaz, who invited her to do all her gleaning on his land, and even to eat with his household. She could not understand why he was so considerate to an alien. He explained: He had heard of her devotion to her mother-in-law, Naomi. He added, "May the Lord reward your conduct . . . the God of Israel, under Whose wings you have come to shelter!"

2:12

For the Rabbis of the Talmud, this last phrase became the standard one to describe converts to Judaism (even though they obviously didn't think God had wings).

Later, at lunch time, Boaz asked her to join him. He also ordered his men to be especially considerate as she gleaned among them.

Ruth brought home a bushel of barley, and when she told Naomi where she had worked, Naomi explained that Boaz was a relative. She advised Ruth to keep right on working in his field and in no other. Ruth did this until the end of the barley and wheat harvest.

Naomi then decided to play at being a matchmaker. She advised Ruth to get into her best clothes and go out to the threshing floor at night, in search of Boaz. (During the harvest, people slept in the fields to save time.) When he lay down there, after having eaten and drunk, she should go to him, "uncover his feet," and lay herself down nearby. Ruth followed these instructions, too. At midnight, Boaz awoke, noticed a woman nearby and asked who she was. Her answer is a bit startling to us: "I am Ruth, your maidservant. Take your maidservant in marriage; for you are next of kin."

3:9

She was not being forward with him. Rather, her request was based on two old customs of the Israelites. One is the levirate or "brother-in-law" rule: When a man died childless his brother was supposed to marry the dead man's widow. Ruth was not quite this closely related to Boaz, but it is possible that, by custom, the practice was extended. The other tradition had to do with the family land. No real estate was ever, in theory, supposed to pass out of the family. Even when the family became poor, as happened to Elimelech, it could only mortgage its land until the Sabbatical year or sell it until the Jubilee year. But only men could own land. In Elimelech's family no men were left, so the nearest relative had the first chance to buy permanent possession of the parcel. Ruth was saying, in effect, "Buy the farm, but I go along with it to continue our family line." This is a little different from either the levirate or land laws of the TORAH, which separate the two ideas; here they are combined, perhaps reflecting an early or special practice.

Stone mill

Boaz was agreeable, but, he pointed out, the way was not clear for him to marry Ruth. There was a kinsman closer to her than Boaz. The matter would have to be discussed with him. Then he sent her back to Naomi with a gift of six measures of barley.

Boaz went to the city gate where all legal business was conducted. There he gathered together ten of the elders of the city as witnesses, and the kinsman. (This is one of the bases of the custom of requiring a *minyan,* a quorum of ten men, before community worship may begin.) The kinsman was told of the land that belonged to Elimelech. He could have it, but he must also marry Ruth. He declined the opportunity. As the official sign of his refusal to exercise his option, he performed an odd ceremony. He removed his shoe and passed it over to Boaz. "Now this was the ancient custom in Israel: To validate any transaction in the right of redemption and its conveyance, the one pulled off his sandal, and gave it

to the other; this was the manner of attesting in Israel."

Our own custom of shaking hands on being introduced might seem equally odd in some parts of the world. But our custom originated in more warlike times. The extended open hand was meant to show that there was no weapon in it and that therefore no harm was intended. We do not know how or where the shoe custom started, or what it was originally intended to convey. Apparently the Biblical author felt the same way, because he explains it as "the ancient custom in Israel." Incidentally, the custom is still followed by Jews who observe the laws of levirate marriage. The Rabbis finally prohibited the brother from marrying his childless former sister-in-law, but he must still release her from her special status. To this day, the official sign is the taking off of his shoe, which is called *chalitzah*.

Boaz then said before the witnesses,

> "I am buying from Naomi all that belonged to Elimelech and all that belonged to Chilion and Mahlon. Also Ruth, the Moabitess, the widow of Mahlon, I am buying to be my wife, in order to restore the name of the dead to his estate, so that the name of the dead may not be cut off from among his relatives nor from the council of his home; you are witnesses today." *4:9-10*

Notice that Boaz said he was "buying" Ruth. This should not surprise us, because as a strictly legal matter, taking a wife was still a formal purchase in those times. Jacob made payment for Rachel and Leah with his labor, and the Prophet Hosea complained about the fact that he had spent fifty shekels to buy his faithless wife. In Rabbinic times, there is no longer an actual transfer of money— only a promise to pay. That was devised as a protection against divorce. The husband did not have to pay on marrying, but he would have to make good his promise if he sought a divorce.

The witnesses wished Boaz well, and he and Ruth were then married. In time they had a son, Obed, and Naomi became his nurse. To set the birth of this child in a kind of historical frame, we are told an important fact in the book's last words: Obed became the father of Jesse, who in turn became the father of David, the greatest king of Israel. From this it can be seen that the great-grandmother *4:22* of David was not born into Judaism. She was originally a Moabite. It can hardly be an accident that the ancestor of Israel's greatest king was not only an alien but from an enemy people.

When Moses married a foreign woman, and his brother and sister reproved him for this, the Lord became very angry and punished Miriam, his sister. In the early Biblical period we would guess that *Numbers 12* it was not uncommon for Jews to marry people of other cultures and religions. As time went by, the wise men of Israel reacted against intermarriages. They feared that the Jews would lose their unique belief in God and the ethical way of life it produced. After the Babylonian Exile, when the Jewish community was quite small, this insularity became very important. Nehemiah, for instance, condemned Jews who had married outside the faith, and made an attempt to stop the practice. As one argument he pointed to the occasional sins of King Solomon. Nehemiah felt that the defects in the character of that wise ruler had resulted from the influence of his pagan wives.

Nehemiah 3:25

Some scholars believe that the BOOK OF RUTH was written shortly after the time of Nehemiah. Perhaps it was written as a kind of reproof against those who judged the alien harshly merely because he was not exactly the same as we are. But whatever the reason, it is an unmistakable plea for tolerance. And the book itself is tolerant. It does not raise its voice to make its point. Its tone is quiet, as if very sure of the truth of what it has to tell us. Of course, the book does not at all mean to say that Moabite idol worship and the low way of life associated with it—child sacrifice, for instance— is just as good as the Hebrew belief in the God of Righteousness. That would be carrying tolerance too far. As in the BOOK OF DANIEL, the non-Jew sees the truth of Jewish belief and comes to accept it. What the BOOK OF RUTH is arguing against, then, is the assumption that you have to be *born* a Jew if you are to be considered an acceptable member of the Jewish people. This ageless tale makes the point that belief is as important as birth. Because Ruth believes what Jews believe, because she wants to live as a Jew, because she stakes her life on it, she is welcomed, no matter what her origin. It is not what she was but what she has become that counts. And that point is driven home by giving her a personal share in King David, and, by implication, the Messiah, who shall be a descendant of his family.

The meaning of the story

Each of us has had the experience of meeting briefly someone who makes an impression on us that is unforgettable. The story of RUTH is like such a person. It is only four chapters long. Most other stories in the Bible, like ESTHER, are presented to us as history; some come as part of prophecy. RUTH presents no special credentials. It is more like a love story, or one of those newspaper features which we call "human interest." The facts themselves are not important at all, in the sweep of more important events, but they carry a beautiful message of great social value. It is the sort of thing one sometimes comes across in the lyrics of today's rock ballads.

In its quiet way, this book makes the point that it is wrong to condemn, sight unseen, all members of a group different from one's own. People should not be outlawed as a class, the story says, and every person, regardless of his background, must be judged as an individual. It is worth remembering that in the beginning of this story, Naomi and her family lived for a long time, apparently without difficulty, among people who were not Jews. And then Naomi and her daughter-in-law, who is called the "Moabitess" by Boaz himself, come and live in peace among the Jews.

In many places in the Bible blood flows because of the line that is drawn between peoples. The BOOK OF RUTH treats the same subject with a gentleness and understanding that wins our hearts. It takes for granted that Ruth can give up her Moabite idolatry and throw in her lot with the Jews.

This understanding extends even into a personal area, one that many Americans see as being merely funny. The comedians of this country could barely subsist if they stopped making jokes about their mothers-in-law. But here is a story about a young woman and her mother-in-law that celebrates the love and devotion between them. Remember, Naomi stays home while Ruth goes out to the field to glean and then carries the grain back home. No wonder Boaz comments that everyone knows how good a daughter Ruth has been to Naomi. Even the names of these characters provide us with a special undercurrent of meaning: Ruth probably means "companion," and Naomi means "sweetness."

The Rabbis directed that the BOOK OF RUTH be read in the synagogue at Shavuot. Since a good part of the action takes place during the early harvest, it is an appropriate time of year for the reading. But Shavuot is also the celebration of the making of the Covenant between God and the people of Israel at Mt. Sinai. At our services, the TORAH passage is always the Ten Commandments. That too is a good reason for reading the BOOK OF RUTH then. The Covenant may have been made with the Jews and all who would be born Jewish, but it is not limited to them. Anyone, of any people, may come and take part in it. The author of the BOOK OF RUTH does not doubt that they will come. He wants them to be welcome and so do the Rabbis.

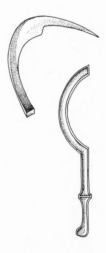

Sickle and scythe

DANIEL

THE POWER OF BELIEF

CHAPTER 4

THROUGHOUT THE FIVE thousand years or so that we know of history, many different peoples have occupied their separate corners of the earth. Of all these, only two have remained relatively intact against the buffetings of time, change, and misfortune. These are the Chinese and the Jews. For the Chinese, the job of persisting in their ancient traditions has been somewhat easier. They have remained always in their same portion of the world, and they have been always a very large population. Foreign invaders, intent on bending the Chinese to an alien will, have become lost, over the years, in all that space and population. They have been absorbed by their intended victim. Today the Chinese, as a people, stand intact.

For the Jews, the job of remaining steadfast to the old ways has been much more difficult. Since the great dispersions, they have been separate wanderers over the earth, some in this part of the world and some in that. They have been denied a sense of geographical unity. And if all the Jews in the world were set down in a country the size of China, they would hardly be noticed. The Jew, unlike the Chinese, has never been able to use his numbers to defy the enemy.

The Jew is a lone, unarmed stranger who has had to travel most of his life through unfriendly and even dangerous neighborhoods. He has usually been, at best, a guest in someone else's homeland. And not a particularly welcome guest, at that. But he has always had one special and not-so-secret weapon to help him survive—his sense that it was right to be a Jew. It is this that has kept him immune to all those fierce pressures which have tried to reshape him in the image of everyone else. The BOOK OF DANIEL is about this kind of perseverance. It tells us what can be achieved if only we believe strongly enough.

The book was written, scholars think, at a time when the Jews were being subjected to great persecutions. It was meant to give them courage and hope, to inspire them to hang on to their faith despite the worst efforts of the enemy. Daniel tells them, in effect, "It is better to die on your feet than to live on your knees." But more than that, he tells them that faith is the secret of continuing to live at all.

Christians consider Daniel one of the Prophets of the Bible. Jews do not. This is because the book talks about the future in a very special style we call "apocalyptic." The word comes from the Greek, and means *to convey a revelation*. In the Bible, apocalyptic writings usually predict dire suffering for the people until an act of God will relieve them of their torment. Often there are strange, even bizarre, visions which convey the message. This kind of writing usually arises in an age of distress, when the faith of the average man is beginning to waver under pressures he finds hard to face. A very few chapters of Isaiah and about half of Zechariah, plus some other random bits of the Bible, can be called apocalyptic.

You and I can find examples of apocalyptic statements all around us. Think of the occasional prophecies of atomic war. On a more homely level, there were the dire predictions, early in 1969, that a great earthquake would level the state of California in April of that year. At least one contemporary religon is based on the idea that the world as we know it will end in this century. It is expected to be replaced by a world much more sensibly run—which should not be too hard to accomplish.

In our Bible we find the BOOK OF DANIEL written partly in Hebrew and partly in Aramaic. The latter language grew out of Hebrew much as present-day English grew out of Anglo-Saxon. Aramaic eventually became the spoken language of the Jews of Palestine. This fact provides us with something of a clue about the origins of the book.

It is probably best to treat the book like a message that has been written in code. On the simple and obvious level, the first half tells a number of interesting stories about some Jews in Babylonia; the second half records some wild visions. To those who can read between the lines, the book presents a message about a period that, to its original readers, was *now.* The *now,* we think, was the time of the Greek tyrant, Antiochus Epiphanes, who ruled over Israel in the days of the Maccabean rebellion, 168 B.C.E.

Let us go back a bit. The Land of Israel was one of the many countries conquered by Alexander the Great. After he died, in 323 B.C.E., his empire was divided into four different kingdoms. Syria was one of these, and Judea was part of it. Over the years in which these Syrian Greeks ruled, many of their customs were introduced among the Jewish people. When Antiochus came to the throne, he stepped up the pace, deliberately imposing Greek influences upon the country. Most Jews resented this invasion of foreign customs, language, and ideas, but there were some who were sympathetic. This naturally produced a great deal of unrest. As with most dictators, the king thought the matter would be simplified if he forced his will on the Jews. A series of anti-Jewish edicts were laid down, in an atmosphere of great turmoil. The climax of this was the desecration of the Temple sanctuary. An idol was placed there for the Jews to worship. This provoked an armed revolt under the leadership of Mattathias, the Hasmonean, and his five sons. Three-and-a-half years later, victory was achieved and the Temple was purged of its defilement. Hanukkah, which means "dedication," is the holiday which celebrates the cleansing of the Temple by the Maccabees.

The BOOK OF DANIEL, it is believed, was written in this period. It is hardly an unusual literary device to take the problems of the present age and present them in the disguise of the past. At the time of Antiochus, the Jews were under the severest pressures to submit to the tyrannizing Greeks. Many, in fact, had chosen the easy way out and had given up their religion. It is not hard to guess what might have happened if all had done the same.

The BOOK OF DANIEL tells a familiar series of stories. In every nation where Jews have been permitted to stay, there have been some who have risen to distinction. This has been true no matter how alien the native culture. Joseph, a slave in Egypt, became the right-hand man of Pharaoh. Maimonides, in the Twelfth Century, became physician at the court of Saladin, ruler of the Arab empire.

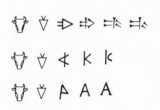

Writing forms

Other examples abound. This book is about one such man, Daniel, and three of his friends.

In his opening words, the writer proves he may not be as good a historian as he is a teacher. He pinpoints the time as the third year of the reign of Jehoiakim, king of Judah, when Nebuchadnezzar led his Babylonian army in the siege of Jerusalem. This would indicate that the year was 606 B.C.E. Many historians believe that Nebuchadnezzar did not rule in Babylon until the following year. But then, the precise facts of Daniel are less important than the ideas.

The first six chapters of the book make one point: the importance of persisting in the Jewish faith despite all trials. Then we get to the climax of the story—visions which are predictions for the future. These are set before us in a symbolic and highly complicated form, and it is not easy to get at their meaning. But throughout this book, it should be realized that though the king may be called Nebuchadnezzar, or Belshazzar, or Darius, the writer is actually concerned about the time of Antiochus Epiphanes. And while he may talk about Daniel or his friends, he really means the whole Jewish people. Keep that code in mind.

Nebuchadnezzar's "Hanging Gardens"

The trials of Daniel

Nebuchadnezzar, we are told in the beginning, had arranged for four handsome and bright Jewish youths to be attached to his palace household. They were to be instructed in "the literature and language of the Chaldeans" and after a training period of three years, *1:4* would be ready for service directly with the king. Daniel was one of those young men, of whom the others were Hananiah, Mishael, and Azariah. (Even the names are a code: Daniel, "My judge is God," Hananiah, "The Lord is gracious," Mishael, probably, "Who is like God?," Azariah, "God is a help." One and all, they stand for the people of Israel.) All their names were changed, however, by royal edict. Daniel became Belteshazzar, while the others became, in order, Shadrach, Meshach, and Abed-nego. You probably recall the spiritual about them.

From the very beginning, the four set themselves apart from the rest of the royal household. They would not eat the food that was forbidden by their own dietary laws. They told their overseer that though they kept strictly *kosher,* they would be perfectly healthy on their own, more limited diet; a brief test period convinced him.

"And at the end of ten days they were better in appearance, and fatter in flesh, than all the youths who ate of the king's delicacies."

1:15

The four were somewhat more intelligent than any of the other young men at the court, and the king got into the habit of conversing with them "in all matters of learning and knowledge . . ." He found them wiser even than the men of magic who served as his regular counselors. They were, in fact, a kind of junior cabinet, or brain trust, for him. We then come to the first real crisis: Nebuchadnezzar had a dream that troubled him very much.

1:20

Now, it is not easy for a professional psychologist to interpret the meaning of a dream even when someone tells it to him. Here, the king made the problem even harder for the "magicians, the enchanters, the sorcerers," on whom he normally depended for such services. He wanted them to tell him exactly *what* he had dreamed, with no coaching from him, before they got around to explaining what it meant. And the penalty for failure was very unpleasant:

2:2

". . . if you do not make known to me the dream and its interpretation, you shall be hewn limb from limb, and your houses shall be made a dunghill."

2:5

The magicians and astrologers were unable to meet the king's terms, and that was the end of all the wise men of Babylon.

Ordinarily, Daniel and his companions would have been included in this mass execution, but Daniel "had a vision in the night" and got word to the king that he would be glad to help in the situation. Just like Joseph, he proceeded to do so.

2:19

The king had dreamed of a mighty statue, made of gold, silver, iron, brass, and clay. It had been shattered by a large stone which in turn became a great mountain. Daniel explained this to mean that Nebuchadnezzar's Babylonian empire would give way to the empire of the Medes. After them would come the Persians, and finally a fourth empire, that of Alexander the Great. This last would be separated into different parts. As for the rock that shattered the statue, it was the kingdom of the God of Daniel—in other words, Judea. This alone was everlasting, because the One True God had chosen it to last for eternity. Daniel told the king that only with the help of this God had he been able to know the dream and unravel it. At this, the king "prostrated himself before Daniel," and

2:46

a sort of conversion took place, for he said, "Truly your God is the God of gods . . . as you have been able to reveal this secret." 2:47

Among other rewards, Daniel was then made governor of all Babylonia. He immediately appointed his friends, Shadrach, Meshach, and Abed-nego to be his assistants. In the matter of the food, and with the dream, faith had been tested and God had seen His faithful ones through.

But the story goes on. It is like one of those old-fashioned thrillers in which the hero is never permitted to rest. He must do many great deeds, any one of which would be sufficient to keep an ordinary man in glorious rewards for a lifetime. The trials of most heroes, however, are physical; think of the labors of Hercules. The ordeals of Daniel were moral.

On most occasions he had only to say Yes to what he did not believe, and his troubles would be over. For instance, the king made an enormous statue of gold, before which he ordered everyone to give homage. Daniel and his three friends refused to do so. The angry king then demanded, "Is it true, O Shadrach, Meshach, and Abednego, that you do not serve my gods . . .?" The king, obviously, had 3:14
reverted to idolatry.

The three young men would not yield, and the king had them bound and thrust into a furnace that was specially heated for the purpose. The heat was so intense that a single flame "slew" a number of the men who were assisting the three victims into the fire. But with the help of God, the three emerged from the flames unharmed. Seeing this, Nebuchadnezzar cried out, somewhat like before,

> "Blessed be the God of Shadrach, Meshach, and Abed-nego, Who has sent His angel to deliver His servants who trusted in Him. . . . Therefore I make a decree that any people, nation, or tongue, that speaks a word against the God of Shadrach, Meshach, and Abed-nego, shall be hewn limb from limb, and their houses made a dunghill; for there is no other god who is able to deliver in this manner." 3:28-29

Note how emphatic the author is. When the Jews keep faith, God will help them. All mankind will then come to see that He alone is truly God.

But the story is not allowed to end here. Most kings, having seen and admitted the power of the One True God on two separate occasions, might have been permanently convinced. But not this one. Once more Nebuchadnezzar had a dream that terrified him. Once more his assembled wise men could make no sense of it. Once more Daniel came forward to explain.

Nebuchadnezzar's madness

This time the king had dreamed of a tree that was so great it could be seen from any part of the earth. But it was cut down, on order from a heavenly being, leaving only a stump. In Daniel's interpretation, the king himself was the tree, and the act of being cut down was a sign that he would endure seven years of madness, after which he would know that the Only True King was God. And that was what came to pass:

4:30

"Forthwith the sentence upon King Nebuchadnezzar was executed. He was driven from among men, and had to eat grass like an ox; his person was drenched by the dew of the heavens, till his hair grew as long as the feathers of an eagle, and his nails as the claws of a bird."

At the end of his seven years of living like an animal, the king's reason returned to him, and he acknowledged the One True God:

4:34

"Now I, Nebuchadnezzar, praise and exalt and honor the King of the Heavens; for all His works are right, and His ways are just; and those who walk in pride He is able to abase."

Several times before, this king had seen the evidence of power superior to his own, and had even admitted it. Yet, after each occasion, he slid back into his old way of thinking, and assumed that he alone was all-powerful. With this latest episode, the story is telling us that power sometimes makes men mad, and when men are mad they are likely to act like animals. Antiochus IV was called Epiphanes because that word expresses what he claimed of himself, that he was "God made manifest." Psychiatrists have written a great deal about the last mad years of Hitler and Stalin. And Lord Acton, the great British historian, put it this way: "Power corrupts; absolute power corrupts absolutely."

The story moves on. Now, we learn, Belshazzar has succeeded Nebuchadnezzar as king. It does not matter that history refuses to confirm this fact. The new king holds a great feast, in the course of which a mysterious hand is seen to chalk a strange message on the wall:

DANIEL

מְנֵא מְנֵא. תְּקֵל וּפַרְסִין:

«MENE MENE, TEKEL UPHARSIN.» 5:25

Once more Daniel does the interpreting. It is a warning to the
new king, he says:

תְּקֵל תְּקִלְתָּא בְמֹאזַנְיָא. וְהִשְׁתְּכַחַתְּ חַסִּיר:

«. . . thou art weighed in the balances,
And art found wanting.» 5:27

Belshazzar's kingdom was destined to be broken up and divided
among the Medes and the Persians.

For his good work, Daniel was now made "third ruler in the kingdom." Rarely has a man been so well rewarded for bringing such 5:29
bad news. That very night, Belshazzar was killed, and his kingdom
passed into the hands of the enemy, the Medes.

The new king was Darius, according to the BOOK OF DANIEL.
According to history it was actually Cyrus. But whoever it was,
he kept Daniel in his high position. The other two members of the
ruling trio were jealous of him, however. They tried to turn the
king against Daniel because of his religion. When Daniel continued
to pray to his God, he broke a law which had been framed specifically to entrap him. The king then had him thrown into a den of
lions. But here again Daniel had the help of the Lord. An angel
kept the lions from annoying him,
    "because he had trusted in his God . . ." 6:23

The king was so impressed by the evidence of Daniel's powers
that he turned on the plotters and had them, along with their families, thrust among the lions. Not believing in the One God, they
were torn to pieces.

Once again, Jewish faith and God's help bring the non-Jew to
see the truth. Darius, too, recognizing the One True God, sends out
a royal decree "that throughout all the kingdom which I rule men
shall tremble in reverence before the God of Daniel;
    For He is the Living God,
    Immutable forever . . ." 6:27

If the story were history we would be bothered by all these instant
and quickly passing conversions. But they are teaching about the
importance of Jewish faithfulness, the help of God and its ultimate
effect upon the nations. Once we know the code, neither the miracles

THE POWER OF BELIEF 53

of furnace nor lions' den seem important. Far more important is the great message these stories brought in the days of Antiochus and bring even today.

The first vision

We now come to the second part of the book. This is the account of Daniel's four apocalyptic visions.

7:1 We learn that he had the first vision while Belshazzar was still king. In it, Daniel saw four strangely shaped beasts come out of the sea. The last of these was the worst, "dreadful and terrible, exceed-

7:7 ingly strong, with great iron teeth . . . and it had ten horns." A small horn rose among these larger ones and began to do great damage. In the midst of this, Daniel saw a "Venerable One" sitting in judgment, after which the fourth beast was slain and burned. The other three were driven away, later to be killed.

Then came a great Messianic vision:

«I saw in the night visions,
And, behold, there came with the clouds of heaven
One like unto a son of man,
And he came even to the Ancient of Days,
And he was brought near before Him.
And there was given him dominion,
And glory, and a kingdom,
That all the peoples, nations, and languages
Should serve him;
His dominion is an everlasting dominion, which shall not pass away,

7:13-14 And his kingdom that which shall not be destroyed.»

The term "son of man" used here seems to mean, simply, one who looked like a man. It later became a term for the Messiah, and Jesus used it often to describe himself.

These matters, and others he saw in the vision, were a riddle to

7:16 Daniel. They were explained by "one of those who stood by."

The four beasts represented four kingdoms: Babylon, the Medes, the Persians, and the Greeks. All of these would give way, eventu-

7:27 ally, to a kingdom "of the people of the saints of the Most High." The little horn that had arisen on the head of the fourth beast, to do so much damage, was of special interest. It foretold the havoc

Figure from Persepolis

that was to be produced by Antiochus IV (although he is never named here). Of him we learn that

> "he shall plan to change the sacred seasons and the law, and they shall be handed over to him for a year, two years, and half a year. Then the court shall take his seat, and his dominion shall be taken away. . . ."   *7:25-26*

Notice that the period of time indicated here adds up to three-and-a-half years. This is the exact period of the Maccabean revolt, after which the tyrant was overthrown. And then God's people, the Jews, received the dominion.

The second vision

This, too, is dated from the time of Belshazzar. In this vision, a *8:1* ram was attacked and killed by a large-horned goat. The goat became very powerful, after which its great horn was broken. In its place came four other horns. Out of one of these four a smaller horn arose, and this

> "became as great as the host of the heavens; and some of the starry host it cast down to the ground and trampled underfoot. It made itself even as great as the prince of the host, whose regular offering was taken away from him, and the site of whose sanctuary was profaned."   *8:10-11*

The angel Gabriel explained all this to Daniel. The ram was the ruler of the empire of the Medes and Persians, while the goat symbolized the Greeks. The goat's large horn represented Alexander the Great, while the four newer horns were meant to be the four kingdoms into which his empire was divided after his death. The smallest horn, the most oppressive, was, we may assume, Antiochus Epiphanes. This vision, Daniel was told, concerned the distant future.

The third vision

In the BOOK OF JEREMIAH, it had been foretold that the Jewish people would have to serve seventy years of captivity in Babylon. Daniel's next vision contemplated this bitter prophecy. While ad- *9:2* mitting the sins of the Jews, he appealed to God to forgive them. As he prayed, the angel Gabriel came to explain to him the meaning of the seventy years. There followed an application of heavenly mathematics that is so complicated people can and have read almost everything into it. It is almost like trying to read the work of a computer that has gone haywire. Specialists on the book have concluded that once more Daniel was being given a symbolic account of the tyrannies of Antiochus before his eventual overthrow.

The fourth vision

10:1 The last vision was by far the longest, and the most difficult to understand. Here again, as in the first two, we get in a symbolic form the same general historical review of those earlier visions. This one, however, offered considerably greater detail. And again it is foretold that someone very much like Antiochus would in good time meet his end in Palestine.

In the final chapter of this book, Daniel is told that when the Archangel Michael would arise eventually,

> «Many of them that sleep in the dust of the earth shall awake, some to everlasting life, and some to reproaches and everlasting abhorrence. And they that are wise shall shine as the brightness of the firmament; and they that turn the many to
12:2-3 righteousness shall be bright as the stars for ever and ever.»

This is one of the few places in the Bible where we are explicitly told the dead will live again. What seems to be foretold is a final day of judgment for the righteous and wicked. Later, the Rabbis will expand this idea and make it a major belief of traditional Judaism.

Daniel is told, at last, to persist in his path until the end. The final lines assure him that after his death he, too, "shall rise to enjoy
12:13 your portion at the end of the days."

The meaning of the story

This book was not written as history or poetry or philosophy. Nor was it written for any of the other reasons which may have brought other portions of the Bible into being. It is more like a battle cry which aims to rally a harassed and battered army. They must "keep the faith" and continue the fight, because the victory is assured. Note the partnership of man and God here. When the Jews do their part, God will help them through great trials. Because God will help them, the Jews should be encouraged to be true to their faith.

Assyrian "scorpion man"

There are historical inaccuracies in many parts of this book. The stories of the trials, in the first six of these chapters, may have been gathered from ancient sources, put together in a package, and ascribed to Daniel. Whether or not they are accurate as history is not as important as the fact that this book has given courage, consolation, and hope to the people of Israel in times when they greatly needed it.

Daniel believed and he persisted in his belief. It is well known that people who believe strongly in something, who, in today's language, are committed to something, stand apart from the mass of men. Their belief is a force. They are far better able to hold their own against a variety of pressures than are those who have no deep belief of any kind. This was especially noticeable during the most terrifying period of contemporary persecution, the years of Hitler. Those who held most strongly to some kind of belief were better able to survive the holocaust.

The importance of this is apparent all around us now, in less obvious circumstances. Many people today don't care very strongly about anything. This lack of commitment is, in a way, a kind of self-betrayal. To take a strong stand *for* something is to affirm that you are also *against* something else. To the extent that you refrain from this kind of affirmation, you are saying that you see no difference between what is right and what is wrong. And in that kind of a moral climate, evil finds it easy to prosper. Men who are great have cared greatly about great ideals. Martin Luther King believed in what he called "a dream." It did not, in the end, protect him from an assassin's bullet. But the power of what he believed enabled him to write his name for all time in the world's brief roster of great and good men.

SONG OF SONGS

A POEM THAT IS ALWAYS MODERN

CHAPTER 5

IF YOU WERE to go to the library, you would discover that more
poems have been written about love than about any other subject.
Most books, movies, and songs deal with it. A major portion of the
world's culture deals with this feeling.

Genesis 2:18   Even the first pages of the Bible deal with love, in a way. After
Adam had made his appearance, God Himself said it was not good
for the first man to be alone. Eve was created, then, to keep him
company. From their very beginnings on earth, man and woman
have completed their creation by finding someone special to live
with. Love is the happy experience of finding your basic loneliness
overcome, of fulfilling your own life by linking it with that of
another. It has taken many forms. Even the cave man, whom we
like to imagine dragging his woman by the hair, is telling his
world, "This is the one I love." From that day to this, love has
been basic to being human.

The SONG OF SONGS is a great poem of love. Does it seem strange
that such a work should be included in the supremely holy book
of a people? Perhaps. But that says more about us and our solemn
concept of religion than it does about Judaism. For the Hebrews,
believing in God was not something limited to going to the Temple
in Jerusalem. That kind of institutional religion is only a minor,
though important, part of the Bible's way of being religious.
Wherever there is life, that is where God and faith need to be.

All through the Bible, men and women suffer and enjoy, they
triumph and they are defeated, they grow enthusiastic, they despair,
and they have periods of hate. How could they leave out the occa-

sions of love? Love is too important an aspect of being human for the Bible not to celebrate it. In the SONG OF SONGS a whole book is dedicated to this most extraordinary and exalting experience.

It should not surprise us that when men set their thoughts to love, the warmest of all human feelings, they express themselves more eloquently than when discussing most other kinds of thinking and feeling and doing. If, on other topics, the Hebrew writers turn to poetry, to exaggerated statement and colorful word-pictures, then how much more should we expect this when they talk about love. A good deal of the SONG OF SONGS flies very high. But a surprising amount is quite simple and almost innocent. Love can be both a raging passion and a tender stillness in one's being. Both moods come out here.

The SONG OF SONGS is a poem or collection of poems about the love that is felt by a young man and a young woman. Scholars have theorized that the occasion is a marriage. The poem talks about the beginning of spring, and if you have ever read much poetry about love, you know the special effect that spring is likely to have on lovers. It is the one season in which all of nature conspires to make us feel particularly fit to be happy. So if the poem was used at marriages or other seasons in the year, those times became springtime for the moment.

If you read the SONG OF SONGS literally, it seems to be a story of King Solomon's marriage to a simple country girl. The very first line, as well as much else in the text, makes this easy to believe. Solomon was a great king, and he permitted himself the luxury of many hundreds of wives. It would not be remarkable to see him playing a major role at this particular wedding. Besides, of him it was written that "his songs were a thousand and five." *I Kings 5:12*

But what is far more likely, in the opinion of scholars, is that this collection of poems which was put together in its present form probably around 250 B.C.E., is a kind of all-purpose wedding bouquet. It was meant to decorate the marriage of any groom and any bride. And if a groom is to be treated like a king on the day of his wedding, what better model than the wise and poetic and powerful Solomon? Even today the bride and groom will dress and celebrate their wedding day with a luxury they normally do not know. They are, so to speak, king and queen for a day. Men often claim that this is rather silly and unreasonable, but most women think it only fitting. In the end, almost everyone seems to find it enjoyable, which is probably why we keep on doing it.

When you read these poems you will notice that in some of them the bride is obviously speaking, while in some it is just as obviously the groom. But in other passages neither one of these appears to be doing the talking, and sometimes we are reading of events which have no connection with love or marriage at all. Scholars have never been able to agree on what is the plan or arrangement of the book as a whole. Some insist there is none, that it is an anthology of many short poems and not one long poem of many parts. So there are few guideposts to help the average reader along the route. That is not really very important. The poetry is so lovely, the phrases so rich, the long sections so moving, that we can simply take them as they come.

The poem

Before you have gone five lines into this poem, you may be struck by how modern it seems to be. The maiden speaking of the kisses of the groom, uses the expression

Grapevine

1:2   "your love is better than wine."

This is the first of many times that you will come across phrases or ideas which have been used in modern poetry or music. This image, in almost the same words, was the theme of a widely played hit song of only a short time ago.

This early on, the wedding has not yet taken place. The bride asks,

"Tell me, you whom I love,
Where you are pasturing your flock,
Where you are making your fold at noon;
For why should I be like one veiled,
1:7   Beside the flocks of your companions?"

If these words mean what they seem to mean, then we would need little other evidence that the SONG OF SONGS is *not* about Solomon. A king of his awesome power would never have found it necessary to herd sheep. Most of the images of the poem, as we shall see, center about the country. There is something about the open fields and the grazing animals that brings out in each of us feelings of tenderness and belonging.

To many Americans, there are few things more strikingly beautiful than a brand-new automobile of graceful design. That is largely because we live in a society in which the machine dominates much of what we do. An Eskimo lives in a world in which his life depends on what he can get from the sea. He might find a seal the most appropriate image of grace and beauty. So the people in this poem, inhabiting a pastoral world of meadows and vineyards, might logically compare the bride to something considered especially marvelous in the country: a fully bedecked thoroughbred horse. Note that it is the great foreign emperor's horse that is described. And like the king it is covered with jewelry:

"To a steed in Pharaoh's chariot,
  I compare you, my love.
  Your cheeks are comely with bangles,
  Your neck with beads.
  Bangles of gold we will make for you,
  With studs of silver."   *1:9-11*

One of the things we may assume from these lines is that precious things have always appealed to people in love. It is their way of saying how dear their love is to them. They give things to their beloved which are choice and rare because they want to express how uniquely valuable they feel their loved one to be. Again and again we see that people haven't changed very much.

Even the language they use hasn't changed a great deal. The SONG OF SONGS glitters with the kind of expressions that everyone feels impelled to use when he is in love. The young man says,

"Ah, you are beautiful, my love;
  Ah, you are beautiful;
  Your eyes are doves."   *1:15*

She speaks of herself as a pretty flower:

"I am a saffron of the plain,
  A hyacinth of the valleys."   *2:1*

He insists she is better than that.

"Like a hyacinth among thistles,
  So is my loved one among the maidens."   *2:2*

«Hark! my beloved!
    ah, here he comes,

Leaping over the mountains,
  skipping over the hills.
My beloved is like a gazelle,
  or a young stag.
Ah, here he stands,
  behind our wall,
Looking through the windows,
  peering through the lattices!
My beloved spoke up, and said to me,
'Rise, my love,
  my beautiful one, come away.'»

2:8-10

כִּי־הִנֵּה הַסְּתָו עָבָר. הַגֶּשֶׁם חָלַף הָלַךְ לוֹ:
הַנִּצָּנִים נִרְאוּ בָאָרֶץ. עֵת הַזָּמִיר הִגִּיעַ.
וְקוֹל הַתּוֹר נִשְׁמַע בְּאַרְצֵנוּ:

«'For, see, the winter is past,
  the rain is over and gone;
The flowers have appeared on the earth,
  the time of song has come;
And the call of the turtledove
  is heard in our land;
The fig tree is putting forth its figs,
  and the blossoming grapevines give forth fragrance.
Rise, my love,
  my beautiful one, come away.
O my dove in the clefts of the rocks,
  in the recesses of the cliffs,
Let me see your form,
  let me hear your voice;
For your voice is sweet,
  and your form is comely.'»

Branch of fig tree

2:11-14

" 'Catch for us the foxes,
  the little foxes,
That are despoiling the vineyards,
  since our vineyards are in bloom.'

2:15

« » The passages enclosed in these special quotation marks, you recall, are recommended for memorizing.

SONG OF SONGS

"My beloved belongs to me, and I to him,
    who is pasturing his flock among the hyacinths.
Until the day blows,
    and the shadows flee,
Gambol, my beloved, like a gazelle
    or a young stag upon the craggy mountains."   *2:16-17*

The poem also contains what seem to be a number of dream sequences. Most of us have had this kind of experience in one way or another. At night, asleep in bed, the mind will often seek out in a dream of someone of whom we are fond. This is nature's way of consoling us for things we may be denied while awake. In the following dream you will notice, the sleeper misses her lover, goes out over the city to look for him, and eventually finds him. In most of the more agreeable dreams, each of us tends to find something that is especially pleasing.

Leaping gazelles

"By night on my bed I sought him whom my soul loveth;
  I sought him, but I found him not.
'I will rise now, and go about the city,
  In the streets and in the broad ways,
  I will seek him whom my soul loveth.'
I sought him, but I found him not.
The watchmen that go about the city found me:
'Saw ye him whom my soul loveth?'
Scarce had I passed from them,
When I found him whom my soul loveth:
I held him, and would not let him go,
Until I had brought him into my mother's house,
And into the chamber of her that conceived me.
'I adjure you, O daughters of Jerusalem,
  By the gazelles, and by the hinds of the field,
  That ye awaken not, nor stir up love,
  Until the time is right.' "   *3:1-5*

A great procession is now described, in which King Solomon approaches with his possessions and his friends. It seems reasonable that it is not really the king. This is only a way of talking about any bridegroom who comes to the celebration with his companions. This passage is one of the reasons for believing that these verses were collected to help celebrate not one wedding but any wedding. *3:6-11*

Now the young man, in a long recital, describes the physical beauty of his loved one. Eyes, hair, teeth, lips, the poem is almost a kind of inventory of the delights of her body. Item by item, in language filled with lush images, the man ticks off the details of his bride's beauty. He is in love, and proud to sing out her glories.

We can understand his delightful exaggeration. When a man is getting married, he is usually brimming over with a sense of pride and joy for the woman he has chosen, out of all others, to be his wife. At such a time it is only natural that he would want to tell everyone just how wonderful she is. What makes this passage stand out for us is, first, the poetic imagination of the author, and, second, the Jewish religious attitude toward sex as a part of love.

Very few bridegrooms in the course of history would be able to think of memorable words and images to describe their loved one. Most bridegrooms, however, have experienced exactly the feelings that the groom here is obviously enjoying. And every bridegroom would want to be able to talk, with this much eloquence, about the way he felt. Like all great poems, the SONG OF SONGS is great for this reason. It expresses a feeling that is common to all mankind.

No less striking is the fact that the body is fully and freely accepted as part of the love. People have often gone to extremes about their love. Some insist it is only something physical, that basically it is our appetite for sex. Others have tried to do away with anything physical in love, insisting that they were concerned with only the spiritual side of their relationship.

Religions, too, have known both extremes. The Canaanites among whom the early Hebrews lived, and even some of the later pagans who surrounded the Jews, were very loose in their sexual standards. They did not connect sex with love so much as with appetite. That is a kind of self-indulgence Jews always thought more suited to animals than to men.

But there were also pagan religions which stressed complete avoidance of sex. So love and sex are important partners, one reinforcing the other. To some people that will seem like a strange subject for religious teaching and for a holy book. But Judaism knows that to serve God is to serve Him with everything important in one's life. So the SONG OF SONGS, with its talk of the body as well as love, is important in Jewish Sacred Scripture. The book is full of passion, and its language fires our thoughts:

«Place me like a seal upon your heart,
    like a seal upon your arm;
For love is stronger than death, as strong as Sheol. . . .
Many waters cannot quench love, nor rivers overcome it,
If one were to offer all the substance of his house for love,
He would be utterly spurned.»   *8:6-7*

Love is not only "stronger than death"; it is usually the strongest thing in our lives. Most men feel an awareness of this on the day they are married. But it is a very rare man who has been able to express that feeling as well as it has been expressed here.

Some useful background

The SONG OF SONGS is a spinning together of many folk poems of love and marriage. And it is all done with great artistry. As a book it is an unsurpassed celebration of the happiest feelings of man and woman for each other. The fact that such a romantic garland could be included in the holiest book of the Jewish religion was a matter of some concern to a number of Rabbis of the First and Second Century. This work was openly passionate, its descriptions of private feeling disconcertingly public. There is no other book like it in the Bible. Therefore it *must* mean something more than it appeared to mean, they felt. It must also be saying something about God and man; otherwise, why include it in the Bible? The early Jewish mystics, with Rabbi Akiva apparently one of the chief advocates, taught that the work was really an allegory. All those heartfelt expressions of love, these interpreters maintained, tell not merely of the love of a man and a woman; we are actually reading about God's love for the Children of Israel.

That was an extraordinary teaching, to see a parallel in the love of man and woman, and the Covenant between God and the Jews. No wonder Jews so cherished the love between husband and wife.

There were other explanations as well. But with all of them, one thing must be emphasized. The SONG OF SONGS also means exactly what it says.

Love and marriage have been a part of life for most of civilized history. And the Bible is, among other things, a story of life and those who live it. It is easy to see, then, the logic of including this celebration of passionate human feelings in this book. After studying its point of view, we should be more surprised if it were omitted.

LAMENTATIONS

THE USES OF DISASTER

CHAPTER 6

SORROW HAS BEEN called a disease for which every patient must treat himself. Long before concentration camps, Czarist pogroms, and medieval Inquisitions, the Jewish people had been struck down with more than one great sorrow. And they had learned to treat themselves for this affliction.

In our own time, we have grown accustomed to mass suffering. In the Twentieth Century there has been plenty of it to go around. Not only Auschwitz, but Biafra; not only Hiroshima and Nagasaki, but Viet Nam. But while we are accustomed to read about awesome troubles in newspapers, magazines, and books, the *poetry* of disaster is rare. Death is not an uncommon theme for poets and the sense of loss is often mentioned, but great social upheavals and apparent national disgrace only rarely make men break into song. And for this kind of poem to become a folk-treasure, a valued memorial of a people, is almost unheard of. Heroes and victory, that is what nations prefer to chant about and remember. The Jews were no exception. But amid their prized books they had one which told of their humiliation, the BOOK OF LAMENTATIONS.

Witnesses frequently disagree about an accident that all have just seen. In the same way, those who endure an identical personal experience may report it in varying ways. Take falling in love, for instance. It can serve as a good example of how people's responses tend to differ. Most people experience love at some time in their lives. When an ordinary person, even someone you are fond of, talks about such an episode, he may make it seem interesting. It would be unlikely, however, to stand out very sharply in your memory. But when a great poet takes the same love affair and lets his genius illuminate it, the result may well stick in your mind for most of your life. That is how the Jewish people has felt about these versions of Jewish catastrophe.

This book of the Bible is composed of five separate poems which bewail the devastation of Jerusalem by an unnamed invader. We know that the Prophet Jeremiah was present at one such invasion. He witnessed the havoc wrought by Nebuchadnezzar, when that king destroyed the Temple of Solomon in 586 B.C.E., and dragged many Jews off to captivity in Babylon. In his book of Prophecy there is an outpouring of sadness and woe over what he sees going on around him. For this reason it was traditional to believe that Jeremiah was the author of these lamentation-poems. But this view is no longer generally believed. In fact, some scholars speculate that a different conquest of Jerusalem is being mourned here. Actually, there is nothing in any passage that refers specifically to the Babylonians.

One conjecture is intriguing enough to deserve mention. It is based on the notion that Jerusalem was sacked a century after Nebuchadnezzar, that is, in 485 B.C.E. At that later time, it is believed, in the first year of the reign of the Persian King Xerxes, the city was overwhelmed by an alliance of surrounding peoples, led by the Edomites. That would explain why, though the Jews had begun coming back from Babylonia in 534 B.C.E., Nehemiah, who came to Jerusalem about 440 B.C.E., found the city wall in ruins. Some verses in the fourth poem point specifically to the Edomites as deserving God's punishment, but it is not clear why. We just cannot be sure who is the actual attacker here.

History often chooses to hand us only a small number of facts about a certain period or event, withholding many others that we might like to know. In this case, there are some things about the background of LAMENTATIONS that are obscured from us. They remain in the dark. What we do know, however, is that these poems, unrelieved in their portrayal of suffering, are undoubtedly the greatest single concentration of poetic grief in the Bible. And their concern is the fate of the nation.

With the opening lines of the first of the five poems, we know we are in the presence of a moment of special disaster:

Bronze lance-head

אֵיכָה יָשְׁבָה בָדָד הָעִיר. רַבָּתִי עָם הָיְתָה כְּאַלְמָנָה.
רַבָּתִי בַגּוֹיִם שָׂרָתִי בַּמְּדִינוֹת. הָיְתָה לָמַס:

"How lonely the city sits,
    once so crowded with people!
She has become like a widow,
    once so great among the nations;
She that was a princess among the cities
    has become a vassal.
She weeps bitterly by night,
    with her tears upon her cheeks;
She has no comforter
    out of all her lovers;
All her friends have betrayed her;
1:1-2   they have become her enemies. . . ."

"Her oppressors have become supreme;
    her enemies have triumphed;
For the Lord has afflicted her
    for the multitude of her sins;
Her children have gone forth,
1:5   as captives before the oppressor. . . ."

«'Ho, all you who pass along the road,
    look and see,
If there is any pain like my pain,
    which has been dealt to me,
With which the Lord has afflicted me
1:12   In the day of His fierce anger.'»

This first poem, in the last stanza quoted here, seems to be calling out to the reader almost from the next building. What is the speaker saying to us, actually? That her agony is so great that nothing in anyone else's experience can possibly equal it. This is understandable when we realize that the sinner, here, feels that God Himself is responsible for this agony.

Everyone knows that there is frequently a kind of vanity about one's own suffering. Most of us have run into it at different times. When we are troubled we feel sure that no one, anywhere, has

68

ever suffered as we are suffering now. The loneliness of what we feel seems to make it more bitter. Yet sometimes, if we are honest about it, we will admit to ourselves that despite the feeling of suffering we also get a certain pleasure in thinking about how unique our situation is.

But the fact is that pain is pain. Some people do feel the same onslaughts more deeply than others, but there are many circumstances in which any human being must suffer to the limits of his endurance. This is true whether the cause is the Warsaw Ghetto, the Siege of Masada, or the death of someone we love. We do not know whether a poetic genius suffers more deeply or whether he is simply able to convey the same pain we feel through an unusually deep imagination.

Here, in these LAMENTATIONS, the pain is expressed to us by men especially gifted in telling us about their feelings. What gives poignancy to their poems is the fact that they believe their unparalleled suffering comes at the hands of God. But they do not blame Him or rail against Him. This is not the BOOK OF JOB. They rather confront us with an honesty that is utterly unexpected. They refuse to look at other people's faults but look at their own. Despite their pain they admit that this is justice for their wrongdoing, that they deserve this punishment. For centuries—at least since Amos, about the year 740 B.C.E.—the Prophets had been warning the Jews that social immorality would bring social destruction. First the Northern Kingdom was destroyed in 622 B.C.E. Then in 586 the Kingdom of Judah was conquered. Like most people, the Jews learned the hard lesson a little too late. But unlike most people, having learned it, they decided to do something about it. The lamentation-poems mark not only the end of one national period but the beginning of another. Social righteousness will now become a continuing Jewish passion, its absence a signal that disaster is near. And every Jewish calamity will be an invitation to self-searching and ethical improvement. In Judaism, disaster becomes a means of instruction.

In the second of these poems, there seems to be no question that the destruction of the holy city, and the misery of its inhabitants, is a just punishment for sin. It tells of the particular horror that comes from the feeling that one has outraged God:

"How the Lord in His anger has brought
        disgrace upon the daughter of Zion!
He has cast down from heaven to earth
        the glory of Israel;
And has given no heed to His footstool
2:1   in the day of His anger."

The images of God's wrath multiply:

"The Lord has become like an enemy;
        He has consumed Israel;
He has consumed all His palaces;
        He has demolished His fortresses;
And He has heaped on the daughter of Judah
2:5   mourning and moaning."

This is not unexpected. There had been Prophets.

"The Lord has done what He planned;
        He has carried out His word,
As He decreed long ago;
        He has devastated without mercy,
And He has let the enemy rejoice over you;
2:17   He has exalted the strength of your oppressors."

And though we expect more exaggeration, the final lines of this
poem are especially terrifying:

". . . But in the day of the Lord's anger
        there was none that escaped or survived;
Those whom I fondled and reared,
2:22   my enemy exterminated."

This poem is written as if Jerusalem, the city herself, were bewailing her own fate.

In the third of these poems of epic despair, the point of view is
somewhat different. Here we are being treated to what we would
call an eyewitness account of the miseries of the event, although
similar images are often used to describe personal troubles in the
PSALMS. For example:

"He has wasted my flesh and my skin;
        He has broken my bones.
He has fenced me in,
        and encompassed me with bitterness and hardship.
He has made me live in the dark,
3:4-6   like those long dead."

But in this third poem there is a glint of hope amid all the misery. It has been a running precept that when one sins, one is duly punished for it by God. True enough. But in Judaism the door is never slammed on the sinner forever. Here we notice that it is kept open to permit the possibility that the sinner will once more make himself worthy of God's favor. God does not punish merely to recompense the evil. No, He wants the sinner to learn from the punishment and turn from that evil way and do the good. That is the great Jewish teaching of *t'shuvah*, "the turning," what we usually call, too weakly, repentance.

> "Let him sit alone in silence,
>> since it has been laid upon him.
> Let him lay his mouth in the dust;
>> perhaps there may be hope;
> Let him offer his cheek to the smiter;
>> let him be sated with disgrace;
> For the Lord will not spurn
>> him forever." 3:28-31

> «Though He cause grief, He will have compassion
>> in accordance with His abundant kindness;
> For He does not willingly afflict
>> nor aggrieve mankind.» 3:32-33

There *is* justice. If you do wrong you will have to pay the consequences. But payment is not the purpose of punishment. Tough as it may be, it does not represent the end of everything. What God really wants of you is righteousness in the future. Normally, punishment comes to show you that you have done wrong. But God is not prejudiced against you because of what you did. He waits for you to begin afresh to do justly and love mercy.

The fourth poem, like the first three, follows the letters of the Hebrew alphabet for each verse. Only here the verses are shorter than in the first three poems. They provide some details about the reason for God's wrath:

> "So the iniquity of the daughter of my people
>> must be greater than the sin of Sodom,
> That was overthrown as in a moment,
>> without any hands being laid on her." 4:6

And also,

"It was for the sins of her Prophets,
the iniquities of her priests,
Who shed in her midst the
blood of the righteous."

4:13

Many of the verses will have, for us, a modern ring. They remind us only too clearly of more recent disasters, with which we are familiar. Few will sound more contemporary than this one:

"Men dog our footsteps,
so that we cannot walk in our public squares;
Our end is near; our days are finished;
for our end has come."

4:18

It sounds almost like Hitler, or a modern police state, or even some of our big cities in which there are neighborhoods where people are afraid to go out at night.

In the last verses of this poem, a warning is thrown out to the people of Edom. Perhaps it is saying, Enjoy your victory, because in God's own good time, you will yourselves endure at least this much suffering:

Gold helmet

"Rejoice and be glad, O daughter of Edom,
living in the land of Uz!
To you shall the cup pass;
you shall become drunk, and be stripped naked.
Your iniquity is absolved, O daughter of Zion;
He will no longer keep you in captivity.
He will punish your iniquity, O daughter of Edom;
He will lay bare your sins."

4:21-22

The final poem is the shortest, and not an alphabetical acrostic. Within its narrower limits it packs just as much torment as the others. Here again, the opening lines seem to bounce from our minds with echoes of contemporary newspapers:

"Mark, O Lord, what has befallen us;
Look, and see our disgrace.
Our heritage has been turned over to aliens,
Our homes to foreigners.
We have become orphans, without a father;
Our mothers are like widows.
Our drinking water we have to buy;
Our wood comes only by purchase.

With a yoke on our necks we are persecuted;
With toil without rest."

5:1-5

These poems have the detailed impact of war communiqués. They seem telegraphed to us directly from the scene of some holocaust. But there is something more important here than the anger of God in destroying Jerusalem and bringing grief to His Chosen People. There is the sense that the victims deserved what they got. God did to them what needed doing, if they were to be brought back to the path of right living. The grief at what is being suffered is only part of the story. It is more than balanced by the sense of guilt. The sin was so great that only the most terrible of punishments was possible—and necessary.

The poems tell us of the downfall of Jerusalem and its people, but even more, they tell us of God's distaste for those who mock the laws of morality. And what is said, finally, is that the way is always clear to reform, that the book is never closed, unalterably, for anyone. Thus, among the last lines, the poet is able to plead,

הֲשִׁיבֵנוּ יְיָ אֵלֶיךָ וְנָשׁוּבָה. חַדֵּשׁ יָמֵינוּ כְּקֶדֶם:

"Restore us, O Lord, to Thyself, so that we may return;
Renew our days as of old. . . ."

5:21

To this day, these words are chanted when, after the reading, the Torah Scroll is returned to the Ark.

Poetry to be heard

Hebrew poetry was not written to be read in silence. It is important to remember this when we read LAMENTATIONS. All the poems of the Bible, from the Prophecies to the PSALMS, were said aloud, memorized and repeated aloud. And they were spoken aloud when people wanted to think or talk about them. There were books in existence, of course, but they were rare. Biblical poetry is meant for the ear rather than the eye.

There is even some reason to think that rather than simply being said, these poems were sort of chanted. This was not quite as formal or musical as synagogue chanting today, but not quite as flat as the simple spoken voice, either. That is particularly true of the poems of LAMENTATIONS. Since there were wailing women whose job it was to chant at funerals, it seems logical to believe that there would be a sing-song poetry of calamity. And since the poems are sad, the tunes—"the dirges"—have a sad cast to them.

Jewish tradition preserves in various countries special mournful chants for reciting the BOOK OF LAMENTATIONS. They have a unique effect upon the hearer. Leonard Bernstein was so moved by the motif that the last movement of his Symphony No. 1, the *Jeremiah,* is a setting of LAMENTATIONS, Chapter 1, and the main musical theme is from a traditional chant for this book.

One can perhaps best get the feel of what this sort of poetry was intended for by thinking of the setting in which the book is now recited. The Rabbis called for it to be read each Ninth of Av, the customary commemoration of the destruction of the Temples and the Expulsion from Spain. At night in the traditional synagogue everything is in a turmoil. Most of the lights are out and only a few candles are lit. The ark is open and empty. Any loose benches or chairs in the sanctuary are turned over. The worshippers sit on low stools or on the floor, as a sign of mourning. These are specific signs and symbols of what the day means. But that is exactly the sort of situation the BOOK OF LAMENTATIONS was written for. Truly to appreciate the book, you should somehow try to imagine yourself chanting it out loud as the tears come down your face.

The Bible provides many examples of how the ancient Jews dealt with the problem of their own suffering, and the BOOK OF LAMENTATIONS is exceeded by none of them. In these brief pages the full measure of woe is presented to us. Unlike what we read in an occasional mournful Psalm, or in the worldly melancholy of ECCLESIASTES, we get here a sense of grief that is unrelieved and total. It is as if the whole world were coming to an end. But Jewish faith knew that could not be.

Jerusalem fell, here, but only for a while. Most of us have, somewhere in our hearts, a different kind of Jerusalem. It can be a belief, a dream, an ideal, a person, or even a thing that is crucially important to us. Sometime, it may crash. When this happens, for whatever reason, it can set up a train of agonies for us. LAMENTATIONS points a lesson for all such disasters, too. The important thing is to see beyond the moment of calamity. We must not stay too long with our defeats. It is enough to learn from them and then go on. For a man of faith, life is a moving forward.

ECCLESIASTES

THE BOOK THAT SAYS NO

CHAPTER 7

IT IS NOT POSSIBLE to lead a life in which there are no disappointments, frustrations, or defeats. The greater the man, in fact, the
greater the likelihood you will discover that difficulties have con-
fronted him. Think of Lincoln and Pasteur, Beethoven and Van
Gogh, or anyone else that you admire. Most of them marched up-
hill through much of their lives—but they never stopped marching.

There are times for every one of us when we are sick while others
remain healthy. If you enjoy feeling sorry for yourself, it will seem
unfair. There are also times when the other fellow gets the prize, the
job, or the girl we want. That too may seem unfair. But all of these
are a normal part of *any* life. Just as we know that "you can't win
them all," sensible persons also know that "you can't lose them all."
To believe, to act, and to talk as if life is all bad or all good is to
show yourself to be quite peculiar.

Now, imagine a man who tells you the story of his life in terms
only of his defeats. He makes a big thing of this, and warns of all
the horrors that are waiting there just for you, too. And imagine
that he talks brilliantly. He is so spellbinding, in fact, that you go
on listening as he tries to pull the rug of hope and joy right out
from under your feet. You may learn a great deal from him. But
when you leave him you will have to strike a balance as to how
much he said is true and how much an odd point of view. Such a
man was the author of ECCLESIASTES.

The writer of these brief and brilliant pages calls himself Kohelet, and the book is so called in Hebrew. Kohelet comes from the

Hebrew word for "community," and Ecclesiastes is simply the Greek translation of this term. These words are not otherwise used. They are often taken to mean "the Preacher," and there is certainly preaching in this book of pessimism and self-doubt. The Preacher's view of life is a bleak one—but never has misery been so beautifully expressed. For centuries, these thoughts have been a special favorite of people who are passing through a period of doubt and disappointment. Where LAMENTATIONS talks about national disaster, Kohelet is saying that one's personal life makes little sense. And he feels that there isn't much that any of us can do to change this.

Canaanite gaming die

Perhaps to insure our confidence in him, the author announces himself as a son of King David. For a time he was assumed to be no less a wise man than Solomon. One tradition says that as a youth Solomon wrote the SONG OF SONGS; when mature, PROVERBS; but when he aged, he wrote ECCLESIASTES. As neat as that thought is, strong arguments against it can be found in the text itself. Most scholars agree that the book as we now have it is very much like the wisdom literature of a later time, perhaps as late as 200 B.C.E. That would place it a generation earlier than the revolt of the Maccabees, a time when the Jews were subject to the rule of the Greeks.

With his earliest words—and they are among his most famous—the author of ECCLESIASTES fires a great blast at the very idea of striving and ambition:

הֲבֵל הֲבָלִים הַכֹּל הָבֶל:

מַה־יִּתְרוֹן לָאָדָם. בְּכָל־עֲמָלוֹ שֶׁיַּעֲמֹל תַּחַת הַשָּׁמֶשׁ:

«. . . Vanity of vanities, all is vanity!
What does a man gain from all his toil

1:2-3   At which he toils beneath the sun?»

We are being told that it is folly to aspire, to work, to want to reach higher in life. And as if he knows that many of us will ask why anyone should believe him, with all his gloomy counsels, he presents his credentials: "I set my mind to search . . . through wisdom everything that is done beneath the heavens. . . . I have seen

1:13-14   everything. . . ."

But only a few lines later, it would appear that even this wisdom he has achieved is hardly worth boasting about: "I set my mind to

knowing wisdom . . . I am convinced this too is striving for the
wind. For with more wisdom is more worry, and increase of knowledge is increase of sorrow." Knowledge is not salvation. Getting a *1:17-18*
Ph.D will not automatically make you wise or happy. He seems
almost to be saying that . . . ignorance is bliss. . . . Most people are
not aware that the full quotation is: "Where ignorance is bliss, 'tis
folly to be wise."

Kohelet tells us something of his life, and it reads like the auto-
biography of someone who has done everything and left nothing
untried. But the result is that he is bored. Worse, nothing makes
any lasting sense. It may be good for a while but in the long run
it is folly. He offers his own bitter experience to convince us of the
uselessness of almost any kind of effort.   *2:1-26*

He is so bitter that he refuses to grant an ultimate distinction
between men and animals:

"All are dust, and all return to dust. Who knows whether the
spirit of man goes upward and whether the spirit of the beast
goes downward to the earth?"   *3:20-21*

What about pleasure?

"I said to myself, Enjoy yourself.
But this also was vanity."   *2:1*

Will money make a difference?

"He who loves money
Will not be satisfied with money. . . ."   *5:9*

And we might as well recognize that

"Just as he emerged from his mother's womb,
Naked does he return, going even as he came;
And he carries away nothing of his toil."   *5:14*

He will not even allow us to believe that things were better in
the "good old days":

"Do not say,
'Why were the former days better than these?'
For it was not out of wisdom
That you have asked about this."   *7:10*

Albert Einstein wrote that "God does not play dice with the
universe." It was a scientist's way of talking about order, and because Einstein was so ethical, perhaps he included justice as well.
For most of this book, the writer thought otherwise. Man's life and
fortunes were not shaped, he wrote, by his character, by the way

he thought and felt and acted, but rather by blind accident, by nothing less than chance. He insisted that

«. . . the race is not to the swift,
Nor the battle to the strong;
Nor is there bread for the wise,
Nor riches for the intelligent,
Nor favor for the scholars;

9:11   But time and chance happen to all of them.»

Men are caught like fish in an "evil net" and trapped "in an evil time as it falls upon them suddenly." But,

מַה־שֶּׁהָיָה הוּא שֶׁיִּהְיֶה. וּמַה־שֶּׁנַּעֲשָׂה הוּא שֶׁיֵּעָשֶׂה.
וְאֵין כָּל־חָדָשׁ תַּחַת הַשָּׁמֶשׁ:

"Whatsoever has been is that which will be;
Whatsoever has been done is that which will be done;
1:9   And there is nothing new under the sun,"

wrote Kohelet in a particularly vivid passage.

This dim view of the world, variations of which we can hear even today, was not new in his own time. It was apparently a standard theme in wisdom books of the Near East. Here are some pessimistic thoughts about life that were found on an Egyptian papyrus. They go back to more than a thousand years before ECCLESIASTES:

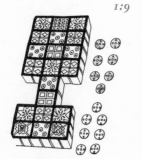

Game board from Ur

> "People are saying, 'We do not know what will happen from day to day.' . . . Great men and small agree in saying, 'Would that I had never been born.' The masses are like timid sheep without a shepherd. . . . Oh, that man could cease to be. . . . Then, at length, the world would find peace."

Kohelet agrees. According to him, "the day of death is better
7:1   than the day of one's birth."

There are a number of things about this author that we can guess from what he writes. He was a man of much learning, no longer young, and he came from what was probably a well-to-do background. He lived in or near Jerusalem, and very likely taught at one of the wisdom academies which were probably common in Greek—that is, Hellenistic—times. Also, it must be remembered, his country was at the time under the control of a foreign empire.

Like Job, Kohelet questioned the conventional idea of God's justice. The fact that known scoundrels can attain great success, while good men flounder in misfortune, disturbed him deeply.

The contradictions of Kohelet

Early in his book, the author expresses a low opinion of the value of human wisdom. Later, echoing the judgment of wise men throughout history, he says that knowledge is power:

> "Wisdom makes a man stronger
> Than the ten rulers who are in the city."

1:17-18

7:19

Immediately after this, he informs us that

אָדָם אֵין צַדִּיק בָּאָרֶץ. אֲשֶׁר יַעֲשֶׂה־טּוֹב וְלֹא יֶחֱטָא:

> "There is no man on earth so righteous
> That he does good and never fails."

7:20

This judgment applies to Kohelet, too. He was certainly wise and no doubt righteous, but there are parts of his wisdom in which he falls down, quite noticeably, before our eyes. For instance, he tells us that "the mind of fools is in the house of mirth," and yet it is not much later that he changes his mind to ". . . I commend mirth; for there is nothing good for man . . . except to eat, drink, and be merry . . ."

7:4

8:15

Although he tells us at one point that it is better to be dead than alive, he later assures us that even a live coward is better than a dead hero:

> "For whosoever is joined to all the living has hope;
> For as a living dog he is better than a dead lion.
> For the living know that they will die;
> But the dead know nothing at all . . ."

9:4-5

In fact, he reserves his greatest contradiction for the twelfth and final chapter of this book. There, having piled the table high with arguments that seem to deny life, he suddenly sweeps everything to the floor:

> «The conclusion of the matter, all having been heard:
> Fear God and keep His commands;
> For this concerns all mankind,
> That God brings every work into judgment
> With regard to everything concealed,
> Whether it be good or evil.»

12:13-14

Many scholars have felt, here, too great a contradiction to be accepted. They believe this was a pious conclusion tacked on by those who wanted to reconcile the book with the rest of the Bible. It is certainly different from everything that came before.

Wisdom for today

Unlike most other parts of the Bible, this one is not written as history, a story, or a poem. It presents to us a series of detached ideas put down in different forms. It is as if someone had been keeping a diary all his life, in which he wrote all that he thought and felt. After his death, the diary was discovered, and the most interesting of these observations were put into a book. Not only do the thoughts appear to skip around from subject to subject, but the outlook is not always the same. Most of the time the writer sees life through darkened glasses, but occasionally he appears to remove the glasses and see things a bit more brightly. He also contradicts himself now and then, a luxury which even the wisest of men have been known to do. But perhaps this is a collection of observations made over many generations, given literary form by one man or school.

In many respects Kohelet is a very modern writer. If some of his comments are translated into a more up-to-date brand of English, they become surprisingly familiar to us. He writes that

"There is one fate for man and beast. . . .

All go to one place; all are from the dust,

3:19-20   And all return to the dust."

In other words, "the paths of glory lead but to the grave."

Even more modern is a comment in which he recommends the value of unity with others. He uses an example which could as well be a plea for the value of labor unions, or the United Nations, as for brotherhood in general:

"Two are better than one,

  for they get a good wage for their toil;

And if they fall,

  the one can lift up his companion.

But if a solitary person falls,

  there is no partner to lift him up. . . .

And if somebody attacks one,

  two can withstand him;

4:9-10, 12   And a threefold cord is not quickly broken."

Fragment of a letter written on clay

And here is another piece of advice that is just as good today as it was in his own time:

"What you vow, fulfill!
It is better that you should not vow
Than that you should vow and not fulfill it.
Let not your mouth bring you into sin,
And say not before the messenger,
'It was a mistake.' "   5:3-5

Or, as President Calvin Coolidge once remarked, "The less you say, the less you have to explain."

Thousands of years ago, the author of this book was aware of the importance of the individual's attitude toward his work:

"Whatsoever your hand finds to do,
Do it with your might. . . ."   9:10

And also,

". . . I saw that there is nothing better
Than that man should rejoice in his work,
Since that is his lot . . ."   3:22

This same idea has been stressed by modern social thinkers: If you choose the right work for yourself, then you should be able to find joy in it. If you cannot enjoy it, then there is something wrong either with you or with the work.

Kohelet tells us many things that would fit very easily into the columns of contemporary newspapers and magazines. Here are just a few of his judgments:

Wealth: It gives no real satisfaction.   5:10-12
Status: The right people are not always in the right positions.   10:6-7
Justice: It is not always available.   3:16
Loneliness: Life is joyless when there is no one who is close   4:8
     to you.

There are many, many more.

The wheel of life

One section of this book is especially famous as a kind of printed balance sheet. Here, some of the ups and downs of life are neatly listed, one against the other, as if to cancel each other out. The   3:1-8
world is a very orderly place, it would seem from this, and everything that one is likely to do must be done only at its appointed time. There is, for example,

"A time to be born, and a time to die;

A time to tear down, and a time to rebuild;

A time to weep, and a time to laugh;

A time to keep quiet, and a time to talk."

These memorable lines help to emphasize the author's theme that man's freedom of will is neither significant nor powerful. But they also make a point, in his own words, which he seems generally to ignore: Life is not all one thing or all the other. It is many things. Only a fool would expect it to be all Yes, and only a desperately unhappy person can see it as all No.

In the first chapter of this book, Kohelet gives us a view of life which was old even in his own time: The sun rises and it sets, and it repeats this pattern over and over, without change. Everything moves in a circle, an unbending and unbreakable pattern, nature seems to say to us. This idea was a familiar one among the Babylonians, the Egyptians, and the Greeks. It is easy to see how such a point of view might give one a feeling of hopelessness about the capacities of mere man. His noblest ideals and actions were made to seem useless. He was like an insect trapped in a great machine that moved round and round without regard for him. Kohelet felt that man could not assert himself against the force of that machine. The best thing for him to do was to let things happen. As far as he is concerned, the workings of fate cannot be affected by the individual's effort. (Men as diverse as Socrates, Mohammed, and Napoleon would laugh at such an idea.)

All the rest of the Bible has another view of man and of time. It pictures man as having significant freedom—that is why God addresses him with commandments. And it sees a direction in history—to the Messianic Age. The idea that history is not cyclical, that it can have a genuine forward movement, was unique to Jewish faith. Through Christianity it became an important part of the distinctive outlook of western man.

In the final chapter of this book we are told, in lines of remarkable beauty and sadness, what it means to be in the twilight of one's life. Talking about one's body and one's feelings, the author draws this picture:

"Remember your Creator in the days of your vigor,

Before the evil days come,

And the years approach of which you will say,

Egyptian irrigation

1:5

ECCLESIASTES

'I have no pleasure in them';
Before the sun becomes dark,
And the light, and the moon, and the stars;
And the clouds return after the rain;
On the day when the guardians of the house tremble,
And the strong men are bent . . .
And those that look out shall be darkened in the windows . . .
And the sound of the bird is faint . . .
And terrors are on the road . . .
Because man is going to his eternal home . . ."   *12:1-5*

When we are old, with our vigor gone, our sense of the joy of life is likely to be greatly diminished. Many of the things that give pleasure, and which we are normally able to take for granted when we are younger, are beyond us in our old age. And this can certainly affect our point of view.

The role of doubt

Pessimism, despair, and the philosophy of doubt have rarely been presented in language as attractive as that of Kohelet. Among the other wise men of his time, the author of such a grim view of life must have been something of a nuisance, if not a heretic. He denied the wisdom of most other men, those who took a more hopeful view of man's ability to shape his own destiny. In this way Kohelet was something of an outlaw. And when he stated, at times, that it was foolish to strive for wisdom, it is possible that his judgment *1:18* was swayed by the difficulties his own thinking may have brought down upon him.

In any society which takes its religion seriously, the number of people who express doubt about the values of that religion is likely to be very small. When such skeptical men write down their doubts, which are in conflict with the accepted thinking of their own time and place, the doubts often get lost. We do not know, for instance, the names of any men of Egypt, Babylon, or Assyria, who might have cast a shadow on the values of their own religion. The sacred books of the world's cultures allow little room for the complaints of the skeptic. But here an official place has been made for skepticism among the most holy books of a people.

ECCLESIASTES is one of the supremely questioning works in the world's literature. Filled with pessimism, it throws beautifully shaped stones at man's belief in his own ability to deal with life. It preaches doubt, despair, and finely phrased hopelessness. No other work can match it for the beauty and subtlety with which it presents the nay-sayer's point of view. It gives us such a fascinating display of thought and language that many readers become almost hypnotized. There are so many rich nuggets of unmistakable truth in this work that they dazzle the reader, making it difficult for him to notice that not everything that glitters before him on these pages is pure gold.

Throughout their long history, the Jewish people have suffered many misfortunes. And yet their literature speaks almost everywhere of hope and the fullness of life. It tells us that man is more than just another living thing; he is a thing apart. He is capable of making a difference in his own life and in his own world, and his actions can be a positive force for good. It might seem that he does not use these special qualities as often as we would like, but no one can deny that they exist. Yet, though this is their faith, the Jews have preserved and honored a book which provides a great and lonely No to this philosophy of affirmation.

In a way, it is good for any society to hear an occasional eloquent voice of doubt. The pessimist and the skeptic serve a useful purpose. They force our attention, even if for only a moment, into the darker corners of the world in which we live. They make us consider the presence of evil, misfortune, and wrongdoing, and keep us from being smug and complacent. It is easy to think we are important. Kohelet reminds us we are nothing. It is easy to get puffed up about what we have done. Kohelet deflates us. It is easy to insist that everyone must do what we do the way we like to do it. Kohelet laughs at us.

The Bible is realistic about life, which is one reason for its greatness. The men who compiled it were aware that in every life there are events and conditions which make war on our idea of the fitness of things. The world is not perfect, and no man has ever celebrated its imperfections as profoundly as the writer of ECCLESIASTES. The fact that his view of life is a part of the Jewish HOLY SCRIPTURES serves as a remarkable tribute to the tolerance, the understanding, and the realism of the Rabbis who decided which books were to be included in the WRITINGS.

EZRA

WHAT THE MAN OF CHARACTER CAN DO

CHAPTER 8

THE BOOK OF EZRA is about loss and about gain. On one level it is about the loss of a place and the return to it. On another, it tells of the loss of a feeling, a spirit, and the recapture of that, too. It is also, of course, about a man.

There are times for each of us when we suddenly realize that our faith in something or someone worthwhile is not what it used to be. It has been slipping away over the years. It may be the special feeling we had for a person, for an ideal, or an idea. The *who* or the *what* is not as important as the sense of loss we are likely to feel. And then along may come some person or event that seems to recharge our batteries for us. Once more we feel the strength that comes from believing in someone or something worthwhile. Ezra was just such a shot in the arm. He was a person, a human being, and in the history of the Jews he was an event. There is nothing mysterious or miraculous about him or his acts. He really lived and we have reliable data about what he did.

Mesopotamian chariot

In 597 B.C.E., the king of Babylon overran Jerusalem and carried 8,000 captives from the city. Eleven years later this same king, Nebuchadnezzar, laid siege to the city again. This time the invaders burned the Temple and took away as many as 50,000 Jews. Those pressed into exile represented every element in Jewish society. They were the rich and the poor, farmers and clerks, laborers and important men of affairs. As has been true of Jews in most countries, some of these rose to positions of eminence, eventually, in their new country.

By the time Cyrus conquered Babylon, later in the same century, many changes had come over the Jewish community there. Those who had arrived in the original group under Nebuchadnezzar were now quite old. They had only the dimmest memories of Jerusalem. Those who had come with the second group brought out by that same king had already been in Babylon for about half a century. Of these two groups, many had taken local women for wives and otherwise succumbed to the customs of the country. And then there was a third group, those who had been born in Babylon. These knew of Jerusalem only by ear. We have only to look around us, in America, to realize that any country, particularly a prosperous and pleasant one, in which the Jews may live for a long time, is likely to produce much the same situation. There are many here, for instance, who have quietly given up on Judaism. They work hard at being part of the general culture.

The BOOK OF EZRA is like a novel in which the hero does not appear until the middle of the story. Only after the first six chapters have set the scene does Ezra make his appearance. Think of it as a tale of war in which a company of men has been leaderless for too long. Undisciplined, mocking all regulations, they are not much fit for battle. Morale is very low. Then a tough new sergeant comes in and straightens everyone out.

But let us get on with the story.

Return from exile

In 538 B.C.E., after the Jews had been in exile for many years, the new ruler over Babylon, Cyrus, king of Persia, issued a decree:

"All the kingdoms of the earth has the Lord . . . given me, and He has commissioned me to build Him a house in Jerusalem,
1:2   which is in Judah."

1:3   «Whoever there is among you of all His people who desires to go, his God be with him; let him go up to Jerusalem . . . .»

Those who remained behind in Babylon were encouraged to support the emigrants with gifts of silver and gold, among other things, for the building of the "house of God which is in Jerusalem." Cyrus himself donated to the expedition those relics of the Temple which had been removed by the victorious Nebuchadnezzar many years before.

This caravan must have been like a city on the march. More than 40,000 people made the trip.

Seven months after they had returned to Jerusalem, the actual rebuilding of the Temple had not yet begun. Many preliminaries had been arranged for, however, and by the second year of the return, the foundation was laid. But there was trouble:

> "Now when the enemies of Judah and Benjamin heard that the exiles were building a Temple for the Lord, the God of Israel, they approached . . . and said . . . 'Let us build with you; for we seek your God, as you do, and we have been sacrificing to Him since the days of Esarhaddon, king of Assyria, who brought us up here.' "

4:1-2

These people, who considered themselves to be Jews, were Samaritans. Their offer—as well as their Jewishness—was rejected by the heads of the families of Israel:

> "You have nothing in common with us . . ."

4:3

The Jews of Jerusalem were a small group and except for their brothers in Babylonia, the only worshippers of One God in the whole world. The Samaritans were originally Assyrian, and had been settled in the old Northern Kingdom a century before. They were, of course, idolaters then. But they felt that in the new country they should worship its God, and they asked for Israelite priests to teach them. Now, a century later, the Samaritan worship of the One God was obviously still mixed with idolatry or otherwise suspect. The refugees who returned to Jerusalem to rebuild Jewish life there had to keep their faith pure and unmixed if it was to survive. It was a time to defend and protect the Jewish vision which the world thought so strange. That concern to keep Judaism alive and honest to itself, despite all the idolatry and paganism round about, is the main theme of this book and its companion, the BOOK OF NEHEMIAH.

King Artaxerxes

The Samaritans then proceeded to take their re   nge. They made all kinds of problems for those who had frozen them out of the building of the Temple. They practiced varieties of sabotage, and also wrote to the Persian king to denounce the Jews. The Jews were rebuilding the city, they warned, perhaps to prepare for rebellion. The Temple, after all, was built like a fort. By this time there was a new king, Artaxerxes, and he was frightened by the report. He ordered the Jews to stop all work immediately.

4:21-22

Later, when Darius became king, the Jews began once more to rebuild the Temple. This was under the leadership of the Prophets Haggai and Zechariah. When the king's emissaries demanded to know by what authority this was being done, the elders of Israel pointed to the original decree of Cyrus, and his special generosities in the rebuilding of Jerusalem.

5:1

King Darius was obviously a stickler for official accuracy. He had the files searched, and sure enough, there was a record of the decree of Cyrus. It even included such details as the specific dimensions to be aimed for in the construction of the new Temple.

6:3-4

Not only did Darius then permit the rebuilding to go ahead, but he encouraged his governor, in the province that contained Jerusalem, to assist with the work:

> "Then the Israelites, the priests, the Levites, and the rest of the returned exiles, celebrated the dedication of this house of God with joy. They offered at the dedication . . . a hundred bulls, two hundred rams, four hundred lambs, and twelve he-goats as a sin-offering for all Israel, according to the number of the tribes of Israel."

6:16-17

Notice the function of those twelve goats. From the custom of selecting an animal to take on the sins of an entire group, we get the word "scapegoat." In more modern times, Hitler chose to use the Jews for this purpose, while in other areas the Negro or the Mexican-American has served. In many places, depending on the prevailing political climate, Communists or anti-Communists have performed this function for the benefit of the majority.

Scribe's materials

Ezra appears

That was the year 516 B.C.E. Our story picks up about seventy years later, when we are introduced to Ezra. The list of his ancestors traces his family back to Aaron, the brother of Moses. He is a priest but we are also told something about him which we have never learned about any Jew before: He was a scribe, skilled in "the Torah of Moses" which the Lord God of Israel had given to the Jews. We have heard of priests and Prophets, elders and judges. This is the first time we hear of a *sofer,* a scribe. All we know about the term is that it has something to do with being learned in the Torah. From what we are told that Ezra did, we can assume it does not mean the writing of new scrolls. It means teaching and leading

7:6

EZRA

people. No wonder, then, that Jewish tradition said that with Ezra the Age of Prophecy ceased and the Age of the Rabbis began. Now the teaching would come not from inspired personalities but from many more educated and intelligent students of the holy books.

When Ezra left Babylon, prepared to rebuild Jerusalem, he carried with him a letter from the king, Artaxerxes, and this letter conferred extraordinary powers upon him. His expedition was made up of about 1,500 Jews, and included many valuable goods. This made it a particularly inviting target for the outlaw bands that roamed the route they were to travel. But Ezra declined to ask for an armed escort. He thought this might make him appear to lack faith, after the way he had described his God:

> ". . . because we had said to the king, 'The hand of our God is with all who seek Him for good, but His power and His wrath are against all who forsake Him.' "

Ezra's faith in the Lord was well placed, and the travelers reached Jerusalem without harm. The year is believed to be 458 B.C.E. It is a time, incidentally, when Greek culture was in the midst of its Golden Age in Athens.

Ezra was shocked by the conditions that he found in Jerusalem, and the thing that shocked him most was the number of Jews who had intermarried with the other peoples in the area.

> "The people of Israel and the priests and the Levites have not separated themselves from the peoples of the lands, and from their idolatrous practices. . . . For they have taken wives from their daughters for themselves and their sons, so that the holy race has mixed itself with the peoples of the lands . . ."

Ezra was so overcome by this that he tore his garment and his mantle, and pulled the hair from his head and his beard, and sat down appalled. Others joined him in mourning, for he was not the only one to realize what would happen to Judaism—and to this tiny community—if Jews continued to marry outside the faith.

The purity of the Jewish religion was in jeopardy, Ezra felt. In his judgment, the act of intermarriage could only result in the loosening of the fibers which held the faith of his fathers together. Nehemiah, some years later, gives us a vivid description of what happened as a result of such marriages:

> "In those days also I saw the Jews who had married women of Ashdod, of Ammon, and of Moab, and their children spoke

7:21-26

8:22

9:1-2

9:3

half in the language of Ashdod, and none of them could speak in the Jews' language, but according to the language of each people."

Ezra put the case for purity in a long speech, of which one paragraph is the key:

"Now after all that has come upon us for our evil deeds and our great guilt, inasmuch as Thou, O our God, hast punished us less than our iniquities deserve, and hast given us a remnant such as this, shall we again break Thy commands . . .?"

A great crowd had gathered, in the meantime, to share in Ezra's grief over these transgressions. Then Shecaniah spoke up, to confess that he, among others, had broken faith with the Lord by marrying a foreign woman. He suggested a "Covenant with God" whereby all who had done this would "put away all the wives

and those born of them."

Ezra proceeded to extract a promise from those present that they would accept this proposal, after which it was done. We may assume that since the Jews, far more than most peoples of the time, had a sense of justice, some arrangement was made to smooth the future for those who had been divorced.

The BOOK OF EZRA closes with a list of those men of Israel who pledged themselves to follow Jewish law and not intermarry. The list is long, but not as long as we might expect in a city that numbered many thousands of people. However, there were many prominent men who had intermarried. Perhaps this was the reason why Ezra felt it necessary to use desperate measures. When a nobody commits a sin, it may mean little to the community at large. When a somebody does the same thing, it is likely to have quite a different effect. Lesser persons in the community take this bad example and now see nothing really wrong in imitating it.

Teaching the people the Law

Bronze idol from Canaan

It was a daring and dramatic thing for Ezra to wage his fight against intermarriage. His greater act, more important in the history of Judaism, and one whose effects lasted much longer, was a positive one. It sounds simple enough but for his time it was a revolution: He read the people the TORAH.

The scene is described for us in the BOOK OF NEHEMIAH, with whom Ezra apparently worked closely. But since it deals with the religious work of Ezra, we must consider it here, lest we fail to see him in proper perspective. It was Rosh Hashanah day. The people were assembled in the broad square before Jerusalem's water gate. Standing on a wooden platform so everyone could see and hear him, Ezra read them "from daylight until midday" the book of the Torah of Moses.

Again and again the description emphasizes to us that the purpose was to get the people to *understand* the TORAH. It was read to

"the assembly of men and women and all that could hear with understanding . . ."

Nehemiah 8:2

"and the ears of the people were attentive to the book of the Law."

Nehemiah 8:3

Various men are mentioned who, with "the Levites instructed the people in the Law. . . ."

וְהַלְוִיִּם מְבִינִים אֶת־הָעָם לַתּוֹרָה. וְהָעָם עַל־עָמְדָם: וַיִּקְרְאוּ בַסֵּפֶר בְּתוֹרַת הָאֱלֹהִים מְפֹרָשׁ. וְשׂוֹם שֶׂכֶל וַיָּבִינוּ בַּמִּקְרָא:

"Thus they read in the book of the Torah of God distinctly, and gave the sense that they understood the reading."

Nehemiah 8:7-8

And in the next sentence the Levites are described as they "who taught the people."

Nehemiah 8:9

The Prophets, you will recall, were not teachers. They denounced and harangued, demonstrated and tried to uplift their hearers. Mostly, their speeches seem to want to smash their way into our skulls. For the Prophets almost everything was an emergency and there was not enough time for patience. God's work must be done *now*.

Ezra, however, is the father of the Jewish thirst for education. He was determined to teach the people, slowly, patiently, not only men but women and any child old enough to understand. He wanted them to know the TORAH—so that they would understand it. Judaism is not a religion for priests or for the Temple. It is a religion for the entire community and every aspect of its life. So the whole community must know the law. How else can one really expect them to observe it?

There is no previous mention in the Bible of reading the TORAH to the people as part of Jewish religious practice. Here there are prayers and ceremonies as the TORAH is read. The Rabbis believed this was the beginning of the later Jewish custom of reading a section of the TORAH in every community on Monday, Thursday, and Saturday mornings. The idea was unheard of in any other religion. A moment's reflection will make clear why. As long as the priests have private and exclusive possession of the holy books, the rest of the people are bound to do what the priests tell them God wants done. The priests have all the power. Let the people know what is in the holy books and the priests can only do what the laws allow. Any learned layman can now argue with them as to what God really wants people to do. The idea of regular TORAH reading makes Judaism a religious democracy. And with it begins the intense Jewish concern for education. For it is not just priests who need to know what the law is. Every Jew needs to know, for it is up to him to keep it. At first that education was oral and for adults. They are the ones who need to be doing what God wants. But in due course it became education in reading, and for children as well.

That is what made the synagogue unique among the religious institutions of mankind. It was as much a house of study as it was a house of rite and prayer. To this day many of the Jewish prayers are more material for the worshipper to study over than to address to God. And of course the reading of the TORAH goes on without a break since Ezra began it so many centuries ago.

The character of the Christian church was decisively shaped by the synagogue. Bible reading is fundamental to it. In the Protestant Reformation, when the Bible was put back in the hands of the people, the old Jewish idea of universal education was spread through western civilization. From it came the modern public school system. In the United States, the Commonwealth of Massachusetts passed its first great education act precisely because it wanted all citizens to be able to read Scripture. Only thus, it was felt, could they outwit "that old deluder Satan," as the law calls him.

There is something incredibly optimistic about this Jewish notion that education will lead to righteousness. It is obvious that many people who know a great deal do very little, that memorizing the Bible will not necessarily make you a good person. True enough. And one should never confuse the good mind with the good will. Yet remember that Jewish education took place inside the Jewish community. What was being taught in the synagogue was being

Clay lamps

largely lived in Jewish families, and by all of them together, as they built their joint way of life wherever they found themselves. The education was very much more effective because it was reinforced by the life the Jews were leading and by the whole range of Jewish ritual and ceremony which touched the heart as well as the mind.

If we are more skeptical today about what schools can do to make people good, it is almost certainly because we expect the school to do the whole job; to teach us what to believe and how to live, while most of the rest of our lives is spent in a reality that confronts us with somewhat different ways of thinking and doing. But is there really any better road to the good life than through education? Is there a more direct way to get men to live a life of decency than to train them for it? Since Ezra's time, the Jews have found no better path than through learning and study, within the community and as part of the total Jewish way of life. Over the centuries, education has served this great purpose for countless generations of our people. That is why the Rabbis could say of Ezra that, had Moses not been worthy to receive the TORAH, God would have undoubtedly given it to Ezra.

The need for an Ezra

Ezra was a scribe, which means apparently something like a scholar of the law, one especially skilled in interpreting the law under the impact of changing times and conditions. In due course, the scribe became the Rabbi.

The role of the scribe, we surmise, was especially important during the years of exile in Babylon. Before that, the Jews were a nation. Their distinct national boundaries helped to set them apart. And they had all the machinery of their own government to encourage their sense of unity. But in exile, the Jews were deprived of such easy grounds for solidarity. The laws and codes of their religion had to carry all the burden of holding them together as a people unique in the sight of God and man. Imagine that we lost a war with China. You and some friends are transported to a large city there, and have to make new lives for yourselves for an unknown number of years, perhaps for the rest of your lives. What would you do, then, to hang onto your sense of yourself as a Jew, an American, an individual? For those who were sent off to Babylon, life was not especially unpleasant. For some, in fact, it was so pleasant that they didn't mind giving up their old dreams and traditions.

The Jews who had returned to Jerusalem seemed in no hurry to rebuild the Temple. They had other things on their minds, if Haggai and Zechariah are right. Those who had been left behind in Jerusalem, and had never tasted exile, were even less enthusiastic Jews. They had been lacking in energy and enterprise. They had done little to build up their community, or even to hold it together. They finally did rebuild the Temple but they certainly did not do much to make their Judaism live.

Caravan

By the time Ezra appeared, nearly a century after the first return, the situation cried out for just such a man as he. He was a born leader, and thoroughly dedicated to the need to uphold Judaic law. His fierce loyalty to this cause came from belief reinforced by the needs of the time. In view of conditions when he arrived on the scene, and given the vigor of his personality, could he have done otherwise? But with the exceptional powers conferred on him by Artaxerxes, he could have played the dictator. He could have forced his will down the throats of the Jews of Jerusalem. He chose instead to convince them by persuasion. He re-established the primacy of "the law," the codes of ritual and conduct that prescribe for every Jew his way of life.

We would call Ezra a reformer. Such men tend to shake up the status quo, forcing many people to change their ways from those to which they have become accustomed. Usually, when this happens, there are those who resent having to make the change from something they are used to, to some way of life that is likely now to be somewhat harder. You can read in the newspapers what happens on any college campus when students demand changes from the administration. But Ezra, for all the toughness of his prescriptions, was able to win the people to his cause.

7:12-26 At first glance it might seem strange that the king should provide Ezra with exceptional powers. But this action becomes easier to understand when we know that the Persian empire was in trouble at the time. There was unrest on many of its borders. The king probably saw a chance to fortify his empire, to the west, by encouraging the Jews to rebuild their city. They were a people of energy and ability, and the ruler could hope to hold their loyalty and support on his frontier.

It is very possible, according to many scholars, that the BOOK OF EZRA was written by the same man (or men) that wrote NEHE-MIAH and CHRONICLES. If so, despite a few puzzling moments here and there, this is a remarkable achievement. There are times in this particular book when Ezra is referred to as "he," while at others he speaks out as "I." It does not matter. And it is odd that we find no mention here of Ezra's great contemporary, Nehemiah. That too does not matter. Perhaps each man wanted to leave his own account of his activities. Occasionally, too, the chronology seems to wander off the historical track as we reconstruct it. We cannot even be sure of the King Artaxerxes to whom the text refers—there were two, in history. All that, too, does not matter.

There is only a single fact, here, that really *does* matter: Ezra rebuilt Judaism, and he did it so well that it still follows the basic direction he gave it.

NEHEMIAH

FAITH PLUS WORK EQUALS A MIRACLE

CHAPTER 9

NEHEMIAH WAS NOT a priest, a Prophet, or a warrior. He was not someone who had obvious qualities for taking command in a crisis of his people. He was more like some man we might see only on Shabbat, at services. He usually sits in the same third-row seat, fourth in from the aisle, and we hardly notice him. But one day he takes charge of the lagging building program for the temple, and suddenly things begin to hum. He seems full of power, as if he had some special authority. We almost are pleased when he tells us what we must do. So everyone talks about him now, as if he were someone quite different from that quiet man we rarely looked at before. And we wonder why we never noticed those qualities that everyone is noticing. We begin to realize, if we think about it, that there are times when it takes an important event to bring out the best in any of us. Think of the boy David suddenly taking on and defeating Goliath.

It is a fact of modern psychology that each of us can probably do more than he thinks he can do. Most of us keep waiting for some special event to turn us into the geniuses we know we are. But it will probably never come, for the truth is we could be doing much more than we are doing right now. When the times *do* make the man, it is the exception rather than the rule. So it was with Nehemiah.

His story is told in the form of a memoir. It is the hero himself who is telling us what happened, and he tells it as a running account of his actions and thoughts. We are able to follow his feelings

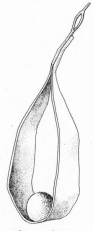

Sling and stone

all the way. This is the first such history available in which a person other than a king tells us what happened, using the form of "I." Before this, the "I" appeared only in a few Egyptian grave inscriptions.

The time that Nehemiah writes about is apparently thirteen years after the changes brought about by Ezra. The earlier man had done his work in reforming the religious life of the people. But a different kind of man was now needed. The community of returnees was small and weak. They were threatened on every side. They were still the only ones in all the world who believed in One God. The time had come for someone who had a grasp of practical affairs and the capacity to enforce his judgments. Nehemiah may never have thought of himself as a leader or hero, but when the challenge came he was just such a man.

The story begins in 445 B.C.E., in the twentieth year of the reign of Artaxerxes, king of Persia. In the royal palace at Susa, Nehemiah, a Jew, was cupbearer to the king. This job was something more than what it may seem to us. It was a position that implied great honor and responsibility, like a Gentleman Usher, for instance, at today's British court. For a Jew descended from a family of exiles brought to Babylon in 586 B.C.E. it was an extraordinary accomplishment.

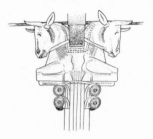

Bull head on column

Nehemiah learned, from some men recently returned from Judea, that things were going badly there.

> "The survivors of the captivity who have remained in Judea are in great misery and reproach. The wall of Jerusalem is broken down and its gates have been destroyed by fire." *1:3*

The news saddened Nehemiah. The king noticed his melancholy and asked the reason. Nehemiah told him: He was troubled by the desperate condition of the city of his fathers. The king, obviously fond of his cupbearer, then gave him permission to go to Jerusalem and rebuild it. But he extracted a promise that Nehemiah would return to the court after the job was finished. He then saw to it that Nehemiah was provided with appropriate authority, and even arranged for him to have timber for the rebuilding program. Unlike Ezra, leader of an earlier expedition to Jerusalem, Nehemiah made the trip with an armed escort.

Three days after he arrived in Jerusalem, Nehemiah made a quiet survey of the situation. With a few followers, he rode one night around the walls, to inspect the great damage which had been done to them and to the gates of the city. He did not even tell the local Jews what he was up to. He probably felt the need for secrecy because he did not wish to give warning to those who might make trouble for him. There were some who stood to profit from an impotent Jerusalem, a situation which is part of today's history, too. Nehemiah was aware that non-Judeans, like Sanballat the Horonite, knew about—and resented—his mission to rebuild the city. Sanballat was something more than just an unpleasant neighbor. He was the governor of Samaria, and not only unfriendly but dangerous. He did not want a strong, somewhat independent Jewish community to the south of him.

Village bake-house

At the time, Jerusalem was only one small part of the Persian empire, surrounded by other parts of that domain. The best way to understand the position of the Jews there is to think of the Land of Israel just before the founding of the present State of Israel. It was then under the rule of the British empire, and the Jews were greatly outnumbered—and disliked—by the peoples around them. But in Nehemiah's time, people were even more uncivilized in international affairs than they are today (or were thirty or forty years ago).

Having finished his survey, Nehemiah gave his report to the Jews of the city:

אַתֶּם רֹאִים הָרָעָה אֲשֶׁר אֲנַחְנוּ בָהּ. אֲשֶׁר יְרוּשָׁלַיִם חֲרֵבָה
וּשְׁעָרֶיהָ נִצְּתוּ בָאֵשׁ. לְכוּ וְנִבְנֶה אֶת־חוֹמַת יְרוּשָׁלַיִם. וְלֹא־
נִהְיֶה עוֹד חֶרְפָּה:

> «You see the serious condition in which we are, how Jerusalem is desolate and its gates are destroyed by fire. Come, let us rebuild the wall of Jerusalem, that we may no longer be an object of reproach.»

2:17

He appealed to them in the name of God, and told them of the goodwill of the king, and his hearers took courage and set to work.

For modern men it is difficult to imagine what it once meant to have a wall around one's city. The obvious advantage was protection. Your enemy could not simply come on his horses and with his chariots and ride right through the midst of your community killing at will. To take a walled city was a major operation, particularly if it was one like Jerusalem, which was up in the mountains and yet had a water supply within the walls.

The less obvious benefit of a wall was what it did for morale. It made a people feel independent. The Jews knew they were still part of the Persian empire but they were no longer going to be forced to do what the surrounding peoples wanted them to do. Having their own secure place, they could also hope to build their own special way of life. The wall was primarily a military matter, but it said a great deal about the boundary between idol-worshipping and the true service of God.

In Judaism one cannot split off the welfare of the Jewish people from the worship of God. Faith and folk go hand in hand. What Ezra had done for the religious life of his people was great. But it was not complete until Nehemiah had assured the future of the Jewish people. The reading of the TORAH was given a future by the building of the wall. Only then could the handful of Jews who had returned to Jerusalem become the basis of the great and creative Jewish community that would arise in Judea in the next few centuries.

Three great successes

Sanballat, meanwhile, went about making warlike threats, trying to frighten the builders, to make them stop their work. This too is a part of modern history. Equally modern is the fact that defense measures were taken to protect the builders from attack, and the work continued. Everyone pitched in, rich and poor, great and humble. Half the workers carried arms, just in case the outsiders should choose to attack.

> "They that builded the wall and they that bore burdens laded themselves, every one with one of his hands wrought in the work, and with the other held his weapon; and the builders, every one had his sword girded by his side, and so builded. And he that sounded the horn was by me." 4:11·12

Again the parallel with modern Israel, where many have been forced to keep one hand on the rifle while the other is on the plow.

After fifty-two days, the Bible tells us, the wall around Jerusalem was rebuilt. This figure raises our eyebrows, in view of the size of the job. Scholars claim that a project that great must have taken years. Perhaps it is only a way of flattering the builders for their zeal and energy. Or perhaps they did not actually complete the job in this amount of time, managing rather to close the last of the gaps in the defenses. The rest of the work could then continue from inside.

Now that he had succeeded in restoring the people's pride by getting them to attend to the wall, Nehemiah turned to other reforms. The Jews of the city had permitted their religious sense to get somewhat rusty. For one thing, many people were violating the Sabbath by doing business on that day. Nehemiah reminded them that the Lord had punished their fathers for just such transgression. He ordered the gates of the city shut just before the Sabbath began, and all the markets, therefore, to be closed. Since there were non-Jews living within the walls now, he also made it a rule that they too should cease from selling on the Sabbath. Here the power of government was being used to make possible the community observance of religion. In a modern country of many different religions, that would not seem harsh, as long as all of them agreed on basic patterns of human decency. But in Nehemiah's world everyone did not believe in the same sort of ethics, even as they did not have the same observances or the same God. And here, again, the wall made possible as nothing else could the development of the unique Jewish way of life.

Nehemiah and Ezra also got the people to agree to observe many of the other customs of the Jewish calendar as set down in the TORAH. The Sabbatical year would be kept, while each year the first fruits of the trees and vines would be brought to the priests in the Temple. The offerings for the priests and Levites were put into proper operation so there could be an appropriate number of singers and servants, doorkeepers and watchmen functioning in the rebuilt sanctuary. There was even a special wood offering by which the people agreed—besides the annual shekel due the Temple—to donate logs so that the sacrifices could be offered.

Another important religious observance had to do with establishing Jewish families so that the Jewish faith might continue. Like Ezra, Nehemiah was bothered by the amount of intermarriage between the Jews and their neighboring tribes. Apparently this practice had taken hold again, despite the original reforms of Ezra. Nehemiah campaigned against it, too. He rebuked those who had married in this way, and demanded that they put away their non-Jewish mates.

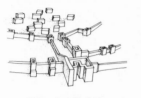
Gate of walled city

13:15-21

10:31-40

NEHEMIAH

All this makes Nehemiah sound somewhat stiff and formal, almost as if he were some sort of school principal who only cares about setting rules and getting them followed strictly. So the third of Nehemiah's great interests will help set the picture right. Just as the wall made possible the religious life, so the concern for following the laws of the TORAH is intimately tied in with a strong sense of ethics. Nehemiah worked to build a just community. He did not do this like the Prophets, by preaching and demonstrating. He was part of the new Jewish style. He did it by teaching, by reminding people of their responsibilities, and, to be sure, by using the power of the law. From now on, Jewish leadership would have to mean a sensitivity to social discontent and a passion for establishing justice.

As often happens, the new triumphs brought new problems. The entire community had locked arms to join in the rebuilding of the wall. This had taken many people away from the jobs by which they usually made their living. Normal work rolled to a halt. Food and goods fell into short supply and prices rose. As a result, many people were no longer able to pay their bills. There were some in the community who took advantage of the situation to profit from the difficulties which now beset the poor. A cry arose among the oppressed: "We are giving our fields, our vineyards, and our houses in pledge that we may secure grain because of the famine." In some   5:3 extreme cases, as was the custom, children had been sold into slavery to meet obligations.

Angered by these things, Nehemiah called a meeting of the wealthy offenders and lectured them on their sins. He pointed out that he, too, was lending to those who had less than he, but was making no profit from it. Abashed, the offenders said they would "make restitution . . . require nothing of them; we will do   5:12 precisely as you say."

In connection with profiteering in general, Nehemiah gave a record of his own modest approach in such matters. He was the king's representative in the area. Like many an important politician of our own day, he therefore had what was, in effect, a license to line his own pockets. The former governors received forty shekels of silver besides bread and wine from the people. But look what he says:

"From the time that I was entitled to be their governor in the land of Judah . . . that is, for twelve years, neither I nor my kinsmen had eaten the bread due the governor."

His was a simple and even austere style of life, in contrast with the greed and self-indulgence of the previous officials.

Why Nehemiah?

There are a number of puzzling questions raised by this book. Through them all runs a paradox.

Historically, this is one of the most reliable and accurate books in the Bible. It says nothing unbelievable and has no miracles. Like Ezra it seems founded on authentic documents. Despite that, many things are not clear. The king, we know, did not hesitate to appoint his cupbearer, Nehemiah, governor of Jerusalem when the occasion arose. He would have been unlikely to do this if Nehemiah were nothing more than an elegant bartender. We do not know how Nehemiah rose this high, but it was enough for the history of Judaism that he did so.

But why did he come to Jerusalem? How was it that the right man came to the right place at the right time? Was it a lucky accident of history? It is more likely that there were some in Jerusalem who realized the necessity for a leader, a man not only with the ability to do the job, but also with the official authority to put his ability to work. Who, then, more logical than a Jew who had risen to eminence at the Persian court, one who had easy audience with the king? This may be one explanation of the way in which Nehemiah found out about conditions in Jerusalem.

". . . as I was in the citadel of Shushan . . . Hanani, one of my kinsmen, came, together with certain men from Judah . . ."

This sounds very much like a special deputation sent off to Susa to get the right man for the job. Even today modern Israel is known to appeal to especially qualified Jews in other countries to provide expert advice when the need is felt. Occasionally we hear of an American professor or industrialist being asked to come there for a year or two to give some special leadership.

When Nehemiah came among the demoralized, spiritless people of Jerusalem, he did not come as a Prophet. He could boast of no direct communication with God. He and Ezra pray to God, but they do not claim that God talks to them. Jewish community leaders now follow the TORAH but do not receive special instruction from God. It is true that Nehemiah came with the power of governor, but that was hardly enough to produce in the Jews the zeal and burning energy which he inspired. He must have had a quality of leadership which went far beyond his title and authority.

We can only guess why the people had stumbled in the path once more, after the great work of Ezra. But when Nehemiah arrived, their spirit had fallen again into darkness, and he brought it once more into the sun. One man, if he is the right one, can do this for many others. In World War II, Churchill did it for the English, and De Gaulle for the French. In our country, Washington and Lincoln, among others, have been able to do it too.

We do not know why Nehemiah is never mentioned in the BOOK OF EZRA, his contemporary. And we do not know why Ezra suddenly appears, out of the blue, only after seven full chapters have gone by here. Aside from their meeting at the great assembly, where the TORAH was read out to the people, both men are silent about their collaborations.

The wall

The wall that Nehemiah restored around Jerusalem was not just a protective fence built of stone. It had a symbolic meaning as well. After that, the people of Israel became more and more the people of the TORAH. Walls make for separateness, and in this sense the one that circled Jerusalem was a symbol of the Jewish tendency to remain as one, "a singular people." And then, as Robert Frost has put it, "Good fences make good neighbors." Foreign influence was kept to a minimum, and though the Jews were a tiny minority, idolatry and the low sort of life it bred did not influence or conquer them. Their exclusiveness became a means to their survival and strength.

Beehive clay huts

There were things about Nehemiah which, to us, are not easy to admire. His attitude toward the Samaritans and Ammonites we might consider too stiff-necked. His use of government power to get people to keep the TORAH is strange to us. And his toughness about intermarriage reminds us of his contemporary, Ezra. But it would be unwise as well as unjust to compare the world of 2,500 years ago with our civilization, which Judaism and Christianity have so largely shaped.

CHRONICLES

WHEN FAITH TAKES FORM

CHAPTER 10

EVERY ONCE IN A WHILE, in history, a great idea comes along to help man to a vision of life better than any he has known before. The idea of justice is one of these. Freedom and democracy are others. A great idea is very rare, and when it shows itself, perceptive men try to make it work permanently for the benefit of mankind. As a rule, in order to accomplish this, the idea has to be made "real." It must be clothed in some form of social machinery—"institutionalized."

The Athenians took the idea of democracy and made it visible in the form of a government. Thus they proved that it could be more than a daydream. Men of goodwill could then see, for all time, that this noble idea could actually work. The concept of democracy has been with us ever since, and many governments today function according to its precepts. It has codes of law, rules of behavior, and ideals that we can aspire to. These are not always lived up to as well as we might like, but they are clearly defined, nevertheless, to remind us what man *should* do. Even a great idea will usually work best only to the extent that human beings make it do so.

Judaism, too, was a new and noble idea. It too, like the idea of democracy, offered man a unique and transcending view of himself. And if Judaism was to take hold in the world, it was necessary not only to set down its precepts on paper—the Bible does that—but it needed a working structure of men and functions to help carry it forward. In the world of political ideas that would mean a government or party or other organization. But Judaism was a new moral and religious idea. It was a breakthrough for man in the way he looked at himself not just within the boundaries of some geographical area, but how he regarded himself for all time. To keep the flame of this idea properly lit, Judaism required teachers, leaders, institutions. Only then could the vision and warmth of this new idea be properly transmitted to the Jewish people over the passage of the centuries.

The central institution of Judaism in Biblical times was the Temple. It was the visible symbol of Jewish thought and feeling about man and his relations with the Invisible God. All the great institutions of later Judaism—the courts, the academies, the synagogue—derive from the Temple. It is not surprising, then, that the Temple is a major concern of the BOOKS OF CHRONICLES.

So, not only the idea of Judaism but the forms taken by that idea, gave it the drive—what we would call the continuity—that have carried it forward over the long highway of history. In the pages of CHRONICLES the special forms of Judaism play a significant role. By the time these pages were written, a kind of ripening, a maturity, had taken place in Jewish religious belief. The voices of the Prophets call out, still, from the past, and all else that has gone before is still important to the Jews. But now a shaping process has taken place, a kind of refining of belief and ritual. King Hezekiah, addressing the priests and Levites, indicates procedures for the affairs of the synagogue in verses which begin:

בָּנַי עַתָּה אַל־תִּשָּׁלוּ. כִּי־בָכֶם בָּחַר יְיָ לַעֲמֹד לְפָנָיו לְשָׁרְתוֹ. וְלִהְיוֹת לוֹ מְשָׁרְתִים וּמַקְטִרִים׃

"My sons, do not now be negligent; for the Lord has chosen you to stand before Him to minister to Him, and that you should be His ministers and burn incense."

II Chronicles 29:11

Next time you go to synagogue perhaps you will be alert to the special way in which the service is conducted, the prayers and the forms of the praying, the instruments and the music and the voices which fill the heart as well as the hall. It adds up to a kind of orchestration of belief. And it is in this part of the Bible that we notice the beginnings of these special modes of worship. They did not necessarily *begin* at the time this was written. Long before, they were already a part of the Jewish religion. But it is here that we first read about their history in some detail. Note how the idea of the hymn is brought to our attention:

"Give thanks to the Lord; call upon His name;
Make known His deeds among the peoples!
Sing to Him; sing praises to Him;
Tell of all His wonders!
Glory in His holy name!
May the heart of those who seek the Lord rejoice!
Inquire of the Lord and His might;
Seek His face continually!"

I Chronicles 16:8-11

The FIRST BOOK OF CHRONICLES covers part of the same historical territory as the SECOND BOOK OF SAMUEL, and SECOND CHRONICLES does as much for FIRST and SECOND KINGS. But what we find here, in this later work, is not so much a history as a different view of the events.

And what is that view?

SAMUEL and KINGS give us a sort of political narrative with emphasis on the rulers of the period. This account, in contrast, is a history of the ups and downs of the people's relations with God. It tells of the way He was worshipped and of the Temple and its rituals. And it gives us our first view of the mature shape that the unique beliefs of Judaism had attained in Bible times.

This part of the Bible was written long after the books of SAMUEL and KINGS, and it gets its common name from a Christian saint, Jerome, who lived in the Fourth Century C.E. He referred to these books as "a chronicle of the whole of sacred history." In the Bible, which takes a more matter-of-fact view, they are known as "the events of days."

The troubles of Saul

The first nine chapters of the FIRST BOOK OF CHRONICLES are like a hurry-up survey of Jewish history from Adam to the time of Saul. They are written largely in the form of genealogical tables. The emphasis is primarily on who was related to whom. We would get the same type of history of America, if we had a king instead of a president, and all events were reduced to such matters as births, marriages, and deaths in the royal family.

But this opening section may be making another point, if we only think about it. It encourages the not-so-startling conclusion that all humanity owes existence to one unique root. Regardless of distinctions made by boundaries, color, or belief, every one of us is related to everyone else. We are from the same original stock. And it does not matter that religion and Darwin give different names to that source of all human life, so far away in time. In both cases the judgment is the same: We are all cousins.

In chapter 10, we suddenly witness the death of Saul. He dies by his own hand, one of the rare examples of suicide in the Bible. Judaism is so devoted to life that it considers suicide a sin or a sign of deep sickness. The judgment passed on Saul is interesting:

> "Thus Saul died for his faithlessness wherein he was faithless toward the Lord because of the word of the Lord which he did not observe, and also because he consulted a medium, resorting to it and not to the Lord. Therefore He slew him and turned the kingdom over to David, the son of Jesse."

I Chronicles 10:13-14

Saul had dabbled in the supernatural. In FIRST SAMUEL, chapter 28, he paid a visit to the Witch of Endor. He had asked this medium to raise the Prophet Samuel from the dead, that Saul might get advice concerning his approaching battle with the Philistines. Here he is being condemned for having resorted to magic, as if witches or magicians ruled the world, rather than God. The Bible condemns all such irrational traffic with the supernatural. There is but one God and no formula or potion can hope to control Him.

The times of David

In the very next chapter, David becomes king. He is the center of this FIRST BOOK OF CHRONICLES. It gives us, in its own way, many of the facts we have already learned in earlier portions of the Bible. It tells us too of acts performed by David to bring a greater sense of visible shape and strength to the Jewish religion. In the following verses, for instance, we get an idea not only of the new influence of ritual, but of the joy which suffuses so much of that ritual:

> "Thereupon David made for himself houses in the City of David, and prepared a place for the Ark of God, and pitched a tent for it. Then David said, 'None ought to carry the Ark of God but the Levites; for the Lord chose them to carry the Ark of God and to minister to Him forever.' So David assembled all Israel to Jerusalem, to bring up the Ark of the Lord

to its place, which he had prepared for it. . . . Then David called for Zadok and Abiathar the priests and for the Levites . . . and said to them, 'You are the heads of the families of the Levites; sanctify yourselves, both you and your kinsmen, that you may bring up the Ark of the Lord, the God of Israel, to the place that I have prepared for it. Because you were not ready at the first, the Lord our God broke out upon us, for we did not seek Him in the proper way.' So the priests and Levites sanctified themselves to bring up the Ark of the Lord, the God of Israel; and the members of the Levitical order carried the Ark of God on their shoulders, with the poles, as Moses commanded according to the word of the Lord.

"Then David ordered the chiefs of the Levites to appoint their kinsmen the singers, with instruments of music, lyres, harps, and cymbals who should sound aloud and lift up the voice with gladness. . . .

"So David, with the elders of Israel and the commanders of thousands, went to bring up with gladness the Ark from the house of Obed-edom; and as God helped the Levites who bore the Ark of the Covenant of the Lord, they sacrificed seven bulls and seven rams. . . . Thus all Israel was bringing up the Ark of the Covenant of the Lord, with shouting and with the sound of the cornet and trumpets and cymbals sounding aloud, with lyres and harps. . . ."

I Chronicles 15:1-28

Harp from Ur

David's major ambition, in CHRONICLES, is his desire to build a Temple to God. But God was apparently unwilling to have David erect the Temple. Nathan the Prophet was told to inform the king that this was not to be:

"Go and say to My servant David: Thus says the Lord: 'You shall not build Me a house to dwell in . . . I will make for you a name, like the name of the great who are in the earth. I will also appoint a place for My people Israel and will plant them that they may dwell in their own place . . . and when your days are finished . . . then I will establish your heir after you, who shall be one of your sons, and I will establish his kingdom. He shall build Me a house, and I will establish his throne forever."

I Chronicles 17:4, 8-9, 11-12

David would be permitted to make all the elaborate preparations for the building of the Temple, but the actual construction, it was commanded, would be the work of his son. That is why it is known as the Temple of Solomon.

Sin and consequences

Our government takes a national census every ten years, and each time there are people who refuse to be counted. Some complain about invasion of privacy, some that they have a fear of becoming "a number," and some complain for other reasons. In ancient times, the whole idea of number tended to have a special and even mystical significance to many people. David ran head-on into an aspect of this problem. He decided to take a census of the people of Israel, and this was a great sin. "Now this thing was evil in the sight of God, so that He attacked Israel." David agreed to do penance for his sin. Gad, his special adviser, told him that the Lord was giving him one of three choices:

I Chronicles 21:7

> "Choose either three years of famine or three years of sweeping defeat at the hands of your foes with the sword of your enemies overtaking you; or else that for three days the sword of the Lord and pestilence be in the land . . ."

I Chronicles 21:12

As we can see, none of these offerings was very pleasant. David chose the last, and the pestilence was severe. But God relented, and told the destroying angel to stay its hand.

There is a kind of moral climax to this incident. When David, with his elders, sees the destroying angel with drawn sword, he addresses a plea to God:

> "Is it not I who gave orders to number the people? I am the one who has sinned and done very wickedly; but these sheep, what have they done? O Lord, my God, let Thy hand, I pray Thee, be against me and against my father's house; but not against Thy people that they should be plague-stricken."

I Chronicles 21:17

Most of us who are familiar with history will find this a refreshing point of view for a ruler who has brought trouble upon his people. Kings and emperors, prime ministers and dictators, all kinds of national leaders (even presidents) usually act quite differently when they bring disaster to their country through some personal folly. Rarely does such a leader stick out his neck, at the time of accounting, and admit, "It was all my fault. I'll pay for everything personally." Usually, it is the population at large that is made to pick up the check.

David had done wrong, which is something every one of us does at some time or another. But David was willing to pay for what he had done. This is somewhat rare, not only among rulers, but among ordinary mortals as well. We do not understand why census-taking should seem so evil, but later generations in Bible times had a tradition about David's census and a subsequent plague.

This first portion of CHRONICLES leads us up to the death of David. But just before we get there, we are given a sequence of three chapters, 21, 22, and 23, which provide elaborate details about the building of the Temple. Then David, after having ruled over Israel for forty years, "died at a ripe old age, wealthy and honored,

I Chronicles 29:28

and Solomon his son became king in his stead."

In the first part of CHRONICLES we notice a tendency to idealize King David. He seems relatively faultless, here. The story of his seduction of Bathsheba and killing of Uriah, given us in SAMUEL, is simply omitted. There must be a reason for this, and when we look for it, it is not hard to find. By the time the traditions of this book were written down, the great Prophets were far in the past, and the domination of the Jews by Persia was still very much in being. It was only natural for the Jews, at this time, to let their hearts turn to the greatest of their kings. It was part of the deepening hope of the Jews for a Messiah-King who would lead them once and for all out of the darkness of their suffering. Is it so surprising, then, that at this time their view of him should be touched up here and there by their needs and hopes? This ideal view of David, thrust forward through time, has lighted the way for the Jews through many privations. He is a memory of something great that once was, and represents the hope of what yet may be.

What Solomon prayed for

Every one of the world's cultures hands down, from generation to generation, stories that are meant to teach certain lessons about life. One of these appears, in different guises, in many different countries. It has to do with three wishes. They are usually given to some person by a mysterious stranger. The receiver chooses the wrong things, and what should have brought happiness brings disaster instead. Presumably he has then learned—as the reader and listener are supposed to—that you should think seriously about what you really want in life.

In the first chapter of the SECOND BOOK OF CHRONICLES, God appears to the new king and offers Solomon, in effect, anything he wishes. Solomon replies:

"'. . . Give me now wisdom and knowledge, that I may go out and come in before this people; for who can judge this great people of Thine?'

«Then God said to Solomon,

'Because this was in your mind and you have not asked for riches, wealth, or honor, nor the life of those who hate you, and have not asked for a long life, but have asked wisdom and knowledge for yourself, that you may judge My people over whom I have made you king, wisdom and knowledge are granted to you, and I will give you riches and wealth and honor . . .' »

Luxury pets

II Chronicles 1:10-12

In most such stories, because the wisher chooses unwisely, he loses everything. Here, because Solomon chose well, he was given more than he expected.

In these pages, the story of Solomon's coming to the throne is presented to us in a streamlined version. Also, CHRONICLES pays little attention to the events of the Northern Kingdom which resulted from a rebellion against Solomon's son. The tendency is largely to ignore that area.

Like his father before him, Solomon took a census, but for strictly business reasons. He counted only the "resident aliens" in the land, and large numbers of these were put to work in the building of the Temple. When it was completed, the Lord appeared once more to Solomon, in a dream, and informed him, among other things, that

"if you turn and forsake My statutes and My commands which I have set before you and go and serve other gods and worship them, then will I uproot the people of Israel out of My land which I gave to them, and this house which I have sanctified for Myself I will cast out of My sight . . . and . . . every passer-by shall be amazed and say, 'Why has the Lord done thus to this land and to this house?' Then shall they say, 'Because they forsook the Lord, the God of their fathers . . . and took up with other gods . . .' "

II Chronicles 7:19-22

Once again, by the way, we get the story of that great "summit meeting" when the bountiful Queen of Sheba visits King Solomon.

After a beautiful reign of forty years, the same span as his father, the king dies and is succeeded by his son.

New rulers, new ways

Rehoboam, the new king, did not have, to say the least, the wisdom of Solomon. He will remind many of us of a thoughtless, impulsive young man who inherits a flourishing business, on the death of his father, and proceeds to run it into the ground. Bad advice plus his own bad thinking result in the Northern Kingdom's breaking away from Judah. Matters get worse.

II Chronicles 12:1

> "Now when the kingdom of Rehoboam was established and he was strong, he forsook the law of the Lord and all Israel with him."

There followed an invasion by Shishak, king of Egypt. But because the people of Israel indicated that they realized they had sinned, the Lord prevented the invader from wreaking too much havoc.

Bronze statue of calf

After the death of Rehoboam there was a succession of kings over Israel, many of whom were extremely sinful. In fact, the latter part of CHRONICLES is like a catalog of bad examples of how to live one's life. It spells out many of the horrors of idolatry and evil conduct. But like all bad examples, these are meant to underline for us the importance of moral and social righteousness.

The last chapter of this part of the Bible is one of calamities. First Egypt invades Jerusalem and the son of Josiah is deposed from the throne. Then the Babylonians invade, under Nebuchadnezzar, he who was later to be made to crawl on all fours and eat grass. We are left little doubt about the reason for these disasters that befell Israel:

II Chronicles 36:14

> "Also all the chiefs of the priests and the people proved utterly faithless, in accordance with all the abominations of the nations, and they polluted the house of the Lord . . ."

The result was the catastrophe about which we read earlier in the Bible: captivity in Babylon for a period of seventy years.

Gods, true and false

The message is clear enough. The worship of false gods is bound to bring about destruction. But it would be a mistake for anyone to assume that the Bible is speaking to us only in the directly simple terms that we see at first glance. The lesson, if we spend a bit more time mulling it over, is the same one we are given by modern thinkers: If you devote your mind and your energies to pursuits and values which are fundamentally unworthy of you, then you will pay for it. The Jews who sinned were kept in a physical captivity in Babylon. In our more modern world, anyone who sins against his own spirit is likely to remain captive in another kind of Babylon. The worship of false ideals keeps the spirit in chains.

Finally, in the last two verses of this book, the Jews are released from bondage by the appearance of a noble conqueror, Cyrus, the king of Persia. This was in the Sixth Century B.C.E. Having vanquished Babylon, he permitted the Jews to return to their homeland.

CHRONICLES sets down many details of thought and action that to us are very depressing. But see how this important book ends: The final note is one of optimism, of hope. Like a bugle call, it heralds a return from captivity and the prospect of a new Temple. It is this sense of faith and hope in what is to come that is so encouraging and fortifying a characteristic of the Jewish religion. No matter about the darkness of the *now,* it seems to say to us: stand firm, and tomorrow will be brighter.

The "why" of Chronicles

The last two verses of this book match the first two verses of the BOOK OF EZRA, and some scholars believe that CHRONICLES may in fact have been written by Ezra the Scribe. But we do not know this for sure. We therefore call the author (perhaps he was only a compiler) "the Chronicler," and he probably wrote this work in its present form between 350 B.C.E. and 250 B.C.E. It may have been added to by others later. But the clues of the author's style, as well as his religious and ethical outlook, point to that period.

These two books of the Bible give a new emphasis to events we have read about earlier. In these pages we see Judaism maturing as a religion. The forms of ritual take an enduring shape, and we feel their importance as a unifying element in Jewish life. An institution is being built to carry through the ages the spirit of the Jewish idea of God and man. The Temple no longer exists, but, as with the long-gone Athenian democracy, its memory has given us a noble ideal. And the later temples—the synagogues—have kept Jewish faith and practice alive, despite the dark difficulties of the passing centuries.

JOB

THE MAN WHO ASKED WHY

CHAPTER II

WHEN A BAD MAN comes to a bad end—a Hitler or a Mussolini—
we say he deserved it. Our sense of justice sees that as fitting, and
that is what we mean by saying God is just. But what do we feel
and say when someone who is obviously good—a Martin Luther
King, perhaps—comes to an abrupt and unpleasant end? This is the
problem that has disturbed men who believed that God—in some
places, the gods—were just.

Every human being has had trouble somewhere along the line
of his life. And each of us has known moments of despair when we
have felt a sense of injustice at our misfortune. Sickness may lay
us low for a month, right in the middle of vacation. The house
catches fire. Burglars run off with our valuables. Someone we love
very much dies young. Or a member of the family may be swindled
in a business deal, and the villain goes happily off to Florida. Catastrophe, bad luck, the terrors of chance, suffering, may await us
around any of life's corners. If we believe in a just God, and we
know ourselves to be reasonably good persons, then such troubles
may cause us to wonder: Where is His fairness in all this? Why did
this happen to *me*? Should not the punishment fit the crime?

The customary view of God's justice is as simple to understand
as it was unique in the ancient world. Do good, it says, and you
will have good done to you in your own lifetime. Do evil, and you
will be amply repaid for that, too.

"Behold, the righteous shall be requited in the earth;

Proverbs 11:31   How much more the wicked and the sinner!"

Most religions have some such idea. The sense of justice is universal. What distinguished Judaism was its notion that God's sense of good was not arbitrary. He did not punish or reward out of spite or from playing favorites. Rather He gave men His law, and the heart of that law was not just service to Him and His priests but goodness to men. So a good man—and not just one who gave many sacrifices—should get good from God, here and now.

The BOOK OF JOB raises a powerful voice against this uncomplicated, open-and-shut view. It is a direct challenge to the prevailing doctrine that the good and evil done by each of us will receive its reward and punishment right here on earth. The unknown author of JOB found it hard to believe that this doctrine could be true. Looking around him, he could see—as we do—that there are obvious contradictions. He then set down his resounding doubts in the longest and finest poetic work in the Bible. Filled with imagination and understanding, in language that sparkles with rich images, it is considered one of the greatest works ever penned by man. A soaring theme is expressed here in exalted language.

Centuries ago this book presented the most profound arguments in the debate over the justice of God. The questions it raises about the great Why of human suffering are still with us. Job's ideas cry an alarm against the conventional Jewish thinking of the Fourth Century B.C.E. Why, he wanted to know, does evil exist in a world controlled by an all-powerful God? What reasonable end could be served by permitting good people to suffer? These questions have never been asked with the power and poetry to be found here. And that may be as much of an answer as the book, or any teaching since, has been able to give us. All man can know here is the question, but even to ask it with directness and sensitivity is already to gain great wisdom.

Ecclesiastes, the skeptic, noticed flaws in the way divine justice appeared to operate. Some people, he observed, wouldn't recognize the moral law if they tripped over it on the way to the bank. And yet these people often seem to lead very pleasant lives. But the doubts of Ecclesiastes, while interesting to us, do not arouse the deep feelings that the ideas and poetry of Job provoke.

The BOOK OF JOB is like a great and appetizing sandwich in which the meaty contents stick out from between two thin and scrappy pieces of bread. The containing slices here are a prologue and an epilogue, both in prose. Neither gives us the nourishment of the rich poetic stuff they embrace. The main section is presented to us somewhat like a play, with three separate acts in the form of long speeches of conversation. Each one follows the same order: Job speaks. Then one friend. Job responds. Then another friend. So it goes. There are three cycles of speeches and responses by three friends. The structure is quite clear, though there is a problem at the end of the third round. As with all great drama, when the last curtain comes down there is the feeling that we have experienced something very special. And we have learned something about man and his place in the universe.

Setting the scene

The curtain rises, as we might say, on a most unusual scene for the Bible. God, on His throne in heaven, is receiving from His angels the news of what goes on in the world. One of these angels is named Satan. He is obviously not the Devil of much later literature. He is, as his name implies, an "adversary," or "opponent," but he is perfectly respectful and obedient to God. Satan expresses doubts about a certain man named Job. God thinks very highly of Job, but Satan believes that the man's goodness is only skin-deep.

I:10 "Hast Thou not put a hedge round about him and his house and all that belongs to him?"

Satan believes that God has simply bought Job's devotion by showering good things upon him. Who wouldn't believe, with all those blessings? So God—most strangely—then makes a wager with Satan, giving the adversary permission to put Job's faith to the test. He makes one condition: "Only upon himself you shall not lay

I:12 your hand."

The scene shifts to earth, where Job, up to now the happy and pious head of a fine family, is struck by a series of disasters. His ten children are killed, his flocks and herds are stolen or destroyed, and other misfortunes, as well, fall upon him. When Job receives the news, he utters words which have become a classic utterance in relation to loss:

עָרֹם יָצָתִי מִבֶּטֶן אִמִּי וְעָרֹם אָשׁוּב שָׁמָּה.

יְיָ נָתַן וַיְיָ לָקָח. יְהִי שֵׁם יְיָ מְבֹרָךְ:

בְּכָל־זֹאת לֹא־חָטָא אִיּוֹב. וְלֹא־נָתַן תִּפְלָה לֵאלֹהִים:

«Naked did I come forth from my mother's womb,
  And naked shall I return thither;
  The Lord gave and the Lord has taken away;
  Blessed be the name of the Lord.»   1:21

"Notwithstanding all this, Job did not sin;
  Nor did he charge anything unseemly against God."   1:22
He suffers much, but he does not lose his faith in God. The story, however, has just begun. In life, what seems to be the worst we can stand sometimes turns out to be only the first of our troubles, and so it is with Job.

In the next scene we are once more in the throne room. Satan has failed in his first test of Job's faith, but he complains that the test was not a fair one. Under the original terms, he was forbidden to lay a hand on the person of Job himself. Satan argues that each of us prizes his own body, his own self, more dearly than any possession or any other person. If God were to remove that prohibition, Satan feels, he could quickly corrupt Job. God is sure of Job's piety and permits Satan to proceed to the new test. He lays down, again, only one restriction: "Behold, he is in your power; but preserve his life." Satan then afflicts Job with a severe skin disease, probably boils, "from the sole of his foot to the crown of his head," as the Bible puts it. His fine house gone, Job now sits in a heap of ashes, scraping away at his pained and itching skin with a fragment of pottery. Despite everything, his devotion has remained intact.

Clay model of a house

2:6

2:7

One more pain comes upon him. His wife, embittered by all these disasters, scolds him for his continuing faith in God. That hurts. When we suffer we are helped by the support of those we love. Being deserted and left alone makes us feel worse. Now Job's wife, instead of bringing him comfort, even by keeping silent at his side, turns on him. She whom he loved best fails him when he needed her most. It is one of Satan's cleverest tricks.

Job, however, is as God pictured him. He does not bend before her. Again the response is classic:
  «You speak as the foolish women speak.
    What, shall we receive the good from God
    And shall we not receive the evil?»   2:10
With that, we are ready for the main part of the book, the dialogues.

Three of Job's friends, Eliphaz, Bildad, and Zophar, come to visit, to console Job in his grief. They have trouble recognizing the man they knew, and "tore each his mantle" at what they saw. Completely overcome, they sit down near Job for seven days and nights before anyone speaks.

The drama of doubt

Job finally begins the dialogue. He knows he has been a good man, and he cannot understand why a just God would hurl all this devastation upon him. Bitter and bewildered, he now offers up a great lament, whose tone is set by his opening words:

3:3 "Perish the day wherein I was born . . ."

There are times in anyone's life that are so black that this kind of feeling may take hold for a while. A wall of trouble seems to surround us. It keeps pressing in, depriving the future of any chance of letting the sun into our lives. Usually we have sense enough to know that such feelings are only the mood of a dark but passing period. It was not so with Job. For him things keep getting worse.

"If I entertain a fear, then it comes upon me;
And what I was afraid of befalls me.
I am not at ease, nor am I quiet,

3:25-26 Nor am I at rest; for trouble keeps coming."

He was confused, touched by doubt, but he continued to hang on, to have faith.

Now the first of the three comforters, Eliphaz the Temanite, makes out a kind of case against Job. He insists that God punishes

5:7 only the guilty. "Man is born for trouble," he says, and,

הִנֵּה אַשְׁרֵי אֱנוֹשׁ יוֹכִיחֶנּוּ אֱלוֹהַּ. וּמוּסַר שַׁדַּי אַל־תִּמְאָס:

"Happy, indeed, is the man whom God reproves;

5:17 So do not reject the instruction of the Almighty."

The misfortunes are meant as a lesson, and Job can profit from them. God Himself is the teacher. Therefore, rather than complain, Job should accept his suffering with joy. He must reap what he has sowed. Most of us learn far more truth from our disappointments and suffering than from our successes.

Job will have none of this. He knows that he is innocent of any wrongdoing. But,

". . . the arrows of the Almighty are with me,
And their poison my spirit is drinking;
The terrors of God beset me." 6:4

God has chosen to single him out for disaster. He is powerless to
sway the divine will, whatever the reason behind it. He wants only
to die, and would like God to help him to that end. He is denied
even that last benefit of every troubled human being, the comfort
of sleep:

"When I think my couch may comfort me,
Or my bed relieve my complaint,
Then Thou dost terrify me with dreams,
Thou dost startle me with nightmares." 7:13-14

Many of us have known such nights. He cries out, in language that
touches us all,

"Let me alone! For my days are but a breath,
What is man that Thou shouldst magnify him,
And shouldst set Thy mind upon him,
And shouldst inspect him every morning,
And test him every moment?" 7:16-18

Job's friends are an annoyance, having failed to understand him.
But God should know better. And why does He turn His attention to any only-too-human mortal? How could anyone hope to
stand the scrutiny of the Supreme Being?

In the speech of Bildad the Shuhite, the second of Job's friends,
we realize how shocked they are by what Job has said. Bildad is a
man who has profound faith in the justice of the Lord. He has
just heard Job challenge it, a most reckless thing for any man to
do in any religion. Bildad reasons with Job, pointing out that man
knows very little compared with God, and that if God has chosen
to punish him, then there must be a good reason. Bildad sees Job's
fate as many people would see a bill from the phone company—
the bill is always right.

Job replies to Bildad. His difference with God is a desperately
unfair one, he says. Job is like a man playing in a nightmare card
game. The dealer persists in giving him, by design, only the lowest
cards, and does not even permit him to protest.

"Though I be perfect, He would declare me crooked . . .
The perfect and the wicked He destroys." 9:20, 22

God's justice does not seem to make sense. A man does not stand a chance in contending with it. Job calls up an image here that we can all understand: "O that there were an umpire between us. . . ." And again he asks only that God should leave him alone, that he may have some kind of peace in his last black hours before moving off to the grave.

9:33

Here Zophar the Naamathite speaks. Unlike the other two friends, he does not believe in wasting time on politeness. He is tough, blunt, and even scornful. Job is only a man, he points out, and what can a man hope to understand when faced with an act that is the product of divine wisdom? Man's role is not to reason why but to accept God's judgment on his sins, whatever it may be, and ask forgiveness. In fact, he says, God knows a lot more about Job's sins than is being charged against him. Job is fooling no one by protesting his innocence:

11:2

"Or is a man of ready lips in the right?"

Zophar is making a charge here that could be more generally made in our own era. Nowadays, men caught in some act of public crime or folly will frequently, with "ready lips," cast a veil of innocence over what they have done. And we have all heard of people who seemed to get away with murder only because they were able to hire a clever lawyer or a good public relations man.

Job answers Zophar and his two friends. There is really nothing new in what they have been telling him, he says. It is nothing more than the streetcorner wisdom available from almost anyone to whom he might present his problem. They are only apologizing for the way things are, the status quo. They are not the least bit interested in getting to the bottom of the question he has asked, which is, Why me?

Job is impatient with the windy talk of his friends. He decides on a remarkable means for getting an answer to his question:

"I would speak to the Almighty,

13:3

And I desire to argue with God."

He then goes on to state his case, which is filled with examples of the smallness and weakness of man in contrast to God's greatness:

«Man that is born of woman

Is of few days and full of trouble.

Like a blossom he comes forth and is withered,

And he flees like the shadow and does not endure.

And he wastes away like a rotten thing,
Like a garment which the moth has eaten.
Yet upon such an one Thou openest Thine eye,
And bringest me into judgment with Thyself.»   *14:1-3*

Job is saying that man is only a small, transient thing, here today and gone tomorrow. He is far too insignificant in the scale of eternity to deserve the oppressive attentions that are thrust upon him from on high. The judgment seems out of proportion to the unimportance of man in the general scheme of things. And anyway, exactly why has Job been punished to begin with? He would like to know the specific charges in the indictment against him.

We are now in the second round of speeches. Unlike modern drama, they do not advance the argument much. They only restate it in other terms. That is the way wisdom literature make its points.

God does not answer Job's plea, but Eliphaz does. The tone is tougher: It is about time that Job stopped making so much noise about his own purity. He is only a man, like other men. If he has been punished then it is undoubtedly because he has committed sins. No amount of personal whitewashing will convince anyone otherwise. The heavenly bookkeeper never makes mistakes.

In reply, Job repeats his case, telling again all that God has done to him. But he adds now that he believes the Almighty is aware of his innocence, and will eventually clear Job of having been a sinner. Meanwhile, says Job, he knows that his own death is imminent. It will not be long before he is in the grave, past any opportunity to redeem himself on earth.

Now Bildad presents once more the case against Job. He is untouched by the despair of his unfortunate friend. The language of Bildad is beautiful, the images are striking, but the argument remains pretty much the same: Job is guilty. He should be a decent fellow and own up to his guilt, instead of making a lot of fuss about what a wonderful man he is.

In his first speech to Job, Bildad had thrust at him a shattering argument:

"Does God pervert justice
Or the Almighty pervert the right?"   *8:3*

And it is these almost unanswerable questions that Job now tries to answer.

He appeals to his friend to try to understand that, actually, for whatever reason, an injustice has been done to him. He recites again the horrors visited upon him, and asks his friends to have pity, to try to understand what has happened to him:

"My breath is offensive to my wife,
And I am loathsome to my brothers.
Even the urchins despise me;
If I arise, they speak against me.
All the men of my circle abhor me;
And they whom I loved are turned against me.
My bone cleaveth to my skin and to my flesh,

19:17-20   And I am escaped with the skin of my teeth."

Job cannot guess at the reason why God has chosen to do all this to him, but he is sure that in time he will be vindicated.

We now hear from Zophar again. He offers nothing really new. The same old denunciations are put forward, but now in somewhat different language. When Job answers, he makes a number of bitter observations about the way in which the wicked are occasionally permitted to prosper. He presents an interesting case here for those of us who have wondered why men of obvious evil—gangsters, dictators—are often able to live out the fullness of their lives amid many comforts, surrounded by their loved ones. There is often no visible evidence that such men have ever suffered for their manifest sins.

Job reflects that it is only in death that we find real equality. In that place there is true democracy, because no man there is better or worse than any other. But if the wicked are so obviously able to flourish, Job wants to know, then how can his friends prattle about God's justice in his own case?

This is the third cycle of speeches. Eliphaz now tries to itemize his conception of the charges against Job. Some of these make Job out to be a kind of exploiter of those around him. Other charges appear to be only nit-picking. We do not know where Eliphaz gathered all this information. We were originally told that Job

1:1   "was perfect and upright. He feared God and shunned wickedness." There would seem to be some kind of contradiction here. For all we know, Eliphaz may simply be improvising a case against Job to support his view that punishment derives only from a man's sins.

Job answers, but he does not address himself to the charges of Eliphaz. He dwells more on his wish to confront God. He wants to hear from the Almighty Himself what this is all about.

Now, suddenly, the perfect sequence of speeches breaks off. Chapters 24 through 28 have puzzled scholars for centuries. Chapter 28, for one thing, speaks of the hard road that leads to wisdom. It is a brilliantly written poem. But it does not seem to have any real connection with anything that has gone before in the story. It is like a beautiful blonde child in a family of strikingly lovely brunettes. We appreciate the beauty of the child, but we feel it is too different to belong to such a family. To make some order out of this mix-up, scholars have suggested a rearrangement of chapters, and the reassigning of certain speeches from one character to another. But such suggestions are, after all, only guesses.

In chapters 29, 30, and 31, Job replies apparently to Zophar. He mourns for the happiness he knew in the days before the hand of God fell upon him. In those times he was a mighty man, and people listened to him with respect. His word, then, was like a law to those around him. Now, even the young people do not take him seriously any more:

> "But now they laugh at me,
> Those who are younger than I,
> Whose fathers I disdained
> To set with the dogs of my flock." 30:1

These lines have a curiously modern ring. Many a father of today—though not a Job—is saddened by the same feelings. And most adults are pained that relationships with the young which they could once take for granted are now more strained and difficult.

In chapter 31, Job seeks to justify his life and incidentally presents to us a kind of poetic outline of Jewish ethical ideals.

> "If I set at naught the cause of my male or female slave,
> Then what shall I do when God arises? . . .
> If I withheld aught from the desire of the poor,
> And caused the eyes of the widow to grow dim;
> Or ate my portion alone,
> And the orphan did not eat of it . . .
> If I shook my fist at the orphan,
> Because I saw my help in the gate . . .

Jewelry

If I made gold my confidence,
And called fine gold my trust;
If I rejoiced because my wealth was great,
Or because my hand came upon great riches . . .
If I rejoiced at the calamity of him who hated me,
And was elated when evil came upon him—
I did not let my palate sin

31:13-30

By calling down curses upon him."

Another surprise follows. The next six chapters (32 to 37) give us four speeches by a newcomer named Elihu. He tells Job that he *must* be unrighteous, because God makes no errors in such matters. Besides, punishment is sometimes administered from on high as a form of education, and Job is not facing this possibility with the correct attitude. Job makes a mistake to assume that he can deduce the wisdom of the Almighty; his function is simply to worship Him. God's acts are a warning to Job—he must sin no more.

Many scholars believe this section, too, is an insertion by later hands. This is noticeable in the Hebrew text, because the language is quite different from what surrounds it. Be that as it may, it sets the stage for the climax of the book. Job's request is granted. God speaks to him.

Out of the whirlwind

God's speech is an overwhelming experience. Men have been known to become silent in the face of a judge, a boss, or even a policeman, so it is not hard to understand Job's feelings when God Himself confronts him. With but a brief interruption, chapters 38 through 41 give us the Lord's response. It is as great and sustained a tribute to the wisdom and power of God as is found in all the Bible. It begins this way:

"Then the Lord answered Job from the whirlwind, saying,
Who is this that obscures counsel
By words without knowledge?
Gird up, now, your loins like a man,
That I may question you, and do you instruct Me.
Where were you when I laid the foundations of the earth?
Declare, if you have insight.
Who fixed its measurements, for you should know?
Or who stretched a line over it?

Upon what were its bases sunk,
Or who laid its cornerstone,
When the morning stars sang together,
And all the heavenly beings shouted for joy?
Who enclosed the sea with doors,
When it burst forth, issuing from the womb,
When I made the cloud its covering
And dense darkness its swaddling band;
When I imposed upon it My decree,
And established its barrier and doors;
And said, 'Thus shall you come and no farther,
And here shall your proud waves be stayed'?
Have you ever in your life commanded the morning?
Or assigned its place to the dawn,
That it should lay hold of the corners of the earth,
And the wicked be shaken out of it?"

38:1-13

Man is little and God is great, the Lord points out. How can any human being, from the poverty of his mind, hope to understand the meaning of *everything?* God rules all, and Job, being human, simply cannot understand all that takes place in the world. But it is not necessary for Job to *understand* what God is up to. Rather, what he needs, despite everything, is faith in God's wisdom and justice, even though the way they operate may escape his understanding. One may perhaps say, if he has real faith then no explanation is necessary; if he does not have it, then no explanation is possible.

Job has not actually received a direct answer to his original question: Why am I being punished? But what he does achieve, through the statement of God, is a strengthening of his faith. This is sufficient to give him a sense of peace.

"Therefore I have declared, without understanding,
Things too wonderful for me, without knowing."

42:3

«I had heard of Thee by the hearing of the ear;
But now my eye has seen Thee.
Therefore I retract and repent,
In dust and ashes.»

42:5-6

There follows a brief epilogue in which the Lord tells the friends of Job that they have done a disservice to Him with their preposterous arguments. But they will not be punished, out of regard for "My servant Job." After this, Job is cured of his ailments, and great blessings are heaped upon him. He lives a long and full life, warmed by the presence of new sons and daughters.

Why Job is one of us

It is unlikely that such a person as Job ever actually existed. And the story did not, of course, actually happen. It is simply a portrayal of the ideas which have always bothered men who were concerned about justice. In the Near East, Job's story was familiar as early as the middle of the Sixth Century B.C.E., for Ezekiel mentions him by name. But it was probably told among people who lived even earlier.

To the great question, Why is there evil?, the story has more than one approach.

1. Very early, we get Satan's opinion that a man's goodness is usually fake. It is a kind of window-dressing that is meant to impress others. Misfortune seems to be useful to test the real value of a man's goodness. There is a kind of common sense in this view. Job certainly bends, though he does not crack, under the strain of his afflictions. He goes so far as to question the judgment of God. Yet it is also true that Job is no atheist. He may argue with God, even denounce Him, but he does not deny Him. If he had, there would in a way be no problem, and the whole book would be silly. If God is nasty or merely neutral, then evil is normal and there is no point in complaining about it. Job has a problem—and so do we—only because we know that the idea of goodness is absolutely fundamental to the universe.

2. The argument of Job's friends is the conventional one: Evil and misfortune are necessary penalties. They are put upon us only if we commit sin, do wrong. Job himself would ordinarily like to believe this, but his own experience makes it hard for him to do so. In his misery, he becomes convinced that there is no longer any logic in this view. Reaching deep into the barrel of despair, he plucks out the idea that God may be unjust. But if God is unjust, then we have no complaint against Him. And if justice is only a rare occurrence in the world, or a convenience, we would hardly devote our lives to it. An unjust God would completely change Judaism and alter its way of life. Job may not understand very much at the end, but he understands that his former doubts make

less sense than his faith. He will believe, even though he has great questions.

3. Elihu, the extra voice at the discussion, believes that evil and misfortune are afoot in the world to serve as a warning to us. They provide a form of education and discipline that we ignore at our peril. This point of view, too, offers us something to think about. Imagine a world in which there were never any consequences to doing good or evil. In such a world, it would make no difference what you did. In our world, justice is far from perfect, but that doesn't mean there are no proper consequences to most of what we do. Job is not the rule but the exception. He is a very real problem. But most of us deserve our suffering—a great many of us, far more than we get. The old wisdom is not *always* true, but it is true most of the time.

4. The last explanation is the one provided by God. Evil exists, He tells Job, as a means of letting man know his own ignorance in the face of God's wisdom and power. This answer may leave us a bit dissatisfied and let down. This is because we live in a very precise world of slide rules, computers, and machine tools. Today, every question is supposed to produce a perfectly engineered answer. And in those areas outside the sciences where we have questions, we are ordinarily told that inevitable progress will answer them, too.

Is it really possible to answer *all* questions? Here are a few that even a roomful of scientists would differ on: Does the total universe have limits? And if the answer is Yes, then what lies beyond those limits? If the answer is No, then how can the human imagination conceive of *any* material construction that has no limits whatsoever? What is at the bottom of our ignorance is this: There are some questions thrown at us by the world that require our imagination to grope for answers—and our imagination is only human.

Job is "only human," and that is what God is saying to him. He therefore cannot hope to meet the Almighty on even terms, in any discussion of good and evil. After all, would one of us expect to discuss this matter, as an equal, with a two-year-old brother or sister? There is a wisdom which we cannot know, and to accept it as wisdom becomes a test of our faith. And it is our faith, then, which is all-important. This, Job accepts.

Interestingly enough, modern anthropology makes a related point here. There is a part of life which is cloaked in mystery, de-

Fragment with writing

spite all our probings. Most cultures produce myths to soothe our wonder about such matters. To believe is to achieve an inner peace. But the anthropologists—and the historians—have noticed that when any people begin to question their own myths, the roof seems to fall in on that culture. When the calipers and slide rule of every-day fact are applied to the data of the spirit, the culture apparently begins to decline.

It is clear that the author of the BOOK OF JOB was in revolt against the customary view of God's justice. Neither our sufferings nor our happiness can be completely explained, he felt, as the pay-ment for the way we lead our lives. In fact, this conventional view of God's way with us is almost arrogant: It presumes that God is a justice-machine and must always check each wrong and reward each good deed. That would make man little more than a trained dog. If man's freedom is to mean anything serious, there must be some openness in the way God deals with him.

Nor did the author use the solution to the dilemma which is prevalent in many popular religions: Complete justice comes only in life after death. Biblical Judaism only reached that idea quite late and it may be that its popularity with the Rabbis is partly due to the impact of the BOOK OF JOB.

In discarding the idea that one's good or bad fortunes were auto-matically a visible sign of the judgment of God, the author of JOB provided man with a subtle blessing. No longer would it be nec-essary for man to feel that if his fortunes failed, or if he somehow suffered, he must therefore be making payment for his sins. And on the other hand, anyone who waxed fat and rich could not claim this as a sign of God's favor for his purity of spirit. The view of God's relations with man, as set down in JOB, is from this stand-point a liberating one. It is a brand-new conception of the relation-ship. For one thing, it makes a greater demand on one's faith. That faith is now expected to be completely separated from hope of reward or fear of punishment. This is a considerable advance over that conception in which faith rests on the idea of "What's in it for me?"

In a way, God is pictured as asking honesty-above-all from man. Job's words are angry at times, but his words do express what he really feels. His defiance therefore goes unpunished. But Job's friends, you may note, had to bring sacrifices for speaking so unfeelingly. It would appear from this that the Almighty believes in a kind of free speech. We know that under the pressure of great pain of whatever kind, each of us is likely to cry out in some way that may ordinarily shock. And we are led to believe, here, that God understands. That idea remains in Judaism. What Abraham did, arguing with God over Sodom and Gomorrah, and what Job does here, Jews in later generations have known to be possible for them, too. Only in their religion does one, so directly, question the actions of God. In no other scripture do we read of such a personal confrontation between man and his Creator.

But Job goes one step further:

"Though I be innocent, my mouth would declare me guilty;
Though I be perfect, He would declare me crooked."   9:20

". . . therefore I say,
The perfect and the wicked He destroys."   9:22

God Himself, Job complains, is unable to understand him. This passage, filled with far-out despair, in which Job feels himself beyond the honest notice even of God, represents one of the darkest moments in religious literature. Because if man cannot depend on the awareness and understanding of an all-seeing, all-knowing God, then what is left for him? It is basic to the idea of God that He cares. And yet here Job is persuaded that God has become his enemy. No man who believed in Him could possibly feel lower.

When God finally answers Job, He does not refer to any sins that Job might have committed, or give the answer Job wanted. But in the confrontation with God, Job was granted a stunning honor. His plea to discuss the matter with the Lord had been heard. Now he was given an acute and immediate understanding of the real basis for any valid relationship between man and God: the need for faith, no matter what. The idea is far from any that Job has ever dreamed of, but it makes sense to him. And after he accepts it, the tide turns in his favor.

When we face frustration, defeat, and even perhaps disaster, the reasons are not always easy to understand. Nor do we always face them with heroic calm. That is why the issues brought up by Job in the course of his great dialogues have affected men and women everywhere. But the prologue, which sets the scene for us, seems to make Job almost a puppet, rather than a man thinking out loud against the most prevalent ideas of his time. It makes him out to be not much more than a guinea pig in a laboratory experiment directed from on high. That, as well as the language, is why some scholars consider it a later addition to the book. Without the prologue, Job is one man who questions the moral principles on which the universe operates.

The epilogue too seems to saw off a part of Job's stature as a heroic figure. To us it will seem too pat. If you can only survive your disasters, it apparently says, you will have passed a divine test. You will then acquire more money, fame, and even your family life will become more congenial. But this is the conventional wisdom reasserting itself. Job learned to believe in God despite everything. Now, it seems, such faith will bring you great rewards.

This book, we can see, raises unsettling questions for anyone who accepts the simple view of God's justice as expressed in much of the Bible. But that raises an even greater question: Why was it included as part of Jewish Sacred Scriptures? Perhaps the prologue and epilogue made these disconcerting challenges to prevailing Jewish thought acceptable. Still, why consider them part of God's own wisdom and holy teaching?

The answer would seem to be that though Judaism may not know all the answers, it knows this to be a truly important question, one that is asked over and over, in very many lives. And when we ask it honestly, as Job did, striving for the truth, we perform an act not of heresy but of piety. Job teaches us the way to rebel. He is rebelling against God in the name of justice.

PSALMS

AN ANTHOLOGY OF HUMAN FEELINGS

CHAPTER 12

WHEN YOU OR I feel sad, and express it, it usually comes out in
some familiar stream of words. And should we talk about some
joy or anger that we feel, again the words and thoughts are likely
to sound familiar. It is the same with most of us when we come
to express our confidence or our fear, our love or our shame, or
any other shadings of emotion. When our spirit is aroused for good
or bad, we normally travel over well-worn roads of language in
parading our feelings before the world.

Every great poet has experienced every one of our feelings. But
when *he* has expressed himself, the rest of us have immediately
noticed the difference. With him, what he feels, even if it is one of
the most unpleasant emotions, appears to have been touched with
some kind of special brush. It has become illuminated for all time
by that magic we call "art." And underneath the special beauty of
expression, each of us recognizes the same elemental feeling that
is our own. So it is with the PSALMS.

The ancient Jews, like other peoples, had their moments of sorrow and fear and joy, and all these have been felt by some men
very deeply. The artists among the Jews, three thousand years ago
and perhaps more, turned these passions into poems. For all the
centuries of history, there were poets and singers to make literature
out of some particular mood or event. But there is a great difference
between what we find in the PSALMS and most of the ancient poems
archeologists have discovered.

The PSALMS speak for all men, everywhere, at any time. Christianity has taken them to every part of the world. As a result, to be human anywhere on the earth is to find one's feelings of loss or loneliness, of exultation, fear, and hope, marvelously expressed by Hebrew poets of many, many years ago. The PSALMS have been, for a thousand years and more, like an International Hall of Brotherhood in which the hearts and feelings of all men have been able to meet as one.

These poems may have been born in the specific religious epic of the Jews, but today they are part of the legacy of mankind. Men and women everywhere, in all times, have found consolation, peace, and strength in these lines. There is no extreme of the spirit for which they do not offer some kind of ease. In no other religion is it possible to find a body of sacred literature that can compare with these poems. Ordinary Jews learned many by heart through regular prayer. The most modest of Jewish students read them regularly. They are unique in their capacity to express what it means to have religious feelings, and have thus brought a special depth of feeling into the practice of Judaism. But, like Michelangelo's Sistine Chapel ceiling, at the Vatican, and the church music of Bach, written for Protestants, they belong to everyone.

The BOOK OF PSALMS is now divided into 150 poems or songs or hymns that were written in Israel over a period, probably, of many centuries. Some were no doubt set down very early in the history of the Jews. A good many were probably written after the building of the Second Temple was completed in 516 B.C.E. But it was not till long after that, probably three centuries or so later, that the PSALMS were gathered together into the book we now have, and included in the Bible.

Some of the PSALMS are exclusively concerned with God, while others are more directly personal. Some are almost a social commentary, reminding us of a poetic editorial, or a letter to the local newspaper. As in all collections of poetry, different readers will have different feelings about particular psalms. These poems are not all equally great in quality. Some can stand comparison with the finest works ever set down in writing by man, while others cannot. But as a whole they cast a light that has brightened man's path across the ages.

They have been around a long time, and they are here to stay.

When our astronauts made their first landing on the moon, they left there a number of souvenirs of Earth to commemorate the event. One of these, on a disk, was an extract from a Psalm:

"When I behold Your heavens . . .
The moon and the stars which You have formed;
What is man that You should be mindful of him? . . .
You have made him little less than the angels,
And crowned him with glory and honor.
You have given him rule over the works of Your hands, putting all things under his feet . . ." 8:4-7

Even of such an experience, the PSALMS spoke better than the astronauts knew they could.

The opening chord

Like a great story or poem, a fine movie or play, this book lets you know very quickly that it has something important to say to you. The point that is made in the very first Psalm is one that recurs over and over again in the Bible: It is possible for you to lead the good life; do that, and you achieve a kind of contentment. Choose instead the life of sin and wickedness, and you're in for trouble. You may say to yourself that this kind of message can be delivered to you by any police department. Or by your parents and teachers. But you would be mistaken.

When the Bible recommends the path of right rather than wrong, it is not interested in what the law will do to you. It is interested in *what you will be doing to yourself*. The Norwegian playwright, Ibsen, once wrote that "in this world it is possible for a man to eat well or to sleep well, but it is difficult for the same man to do both." He was overstating the case, but the core of what he meant is clear, even in our own day: If all that you want to do is to "make it," or have your fun, and if, as you hustle along, you trample on other people, what then? You may be able to order the most expensive meal in town, but it may not go down too well. Your uneasy inner life will make it hard for you to do certain things that a reasonably good man can enjoy without feeling uncomfortable. Our judgment begins in our own hearts, or what we usually choose to call "the conscience." But, depending on our sensitivity, it is only an echo of what God thinks of us. We may rule Him out of our lives and insist we do not believe in Him, but He is nevertheless the final measure of what is good and what is evil. And it is under His judgment that we all ultimately stand.

> "How happy is the man who has not walked in the counsel of the wicked,
> Nor stood in the way of sinners,
> Nor sat in the seat of scoffers!
> But his delight is in the Lord's TORAH,
> And in His Law does he study day and night.
> For he is like a tree planted by streams of water,
> That yields its fruit in its season,
> And whose leaf does not wither;
> And whatever it bears comes to maturity.

Winnowing grain

> "The wicked are not so;
> But are like the chaff which the wind drives away.
> Therefore the wicked will not survive the judgment,
> Nor sinners stand in the assembly of the righteous.
> For the Lord knows the way of the righteous.
> But the way of the wicked will perish."

1:1-6

Facing death and loving life

The PSALMS may be poetry, but they are not romantic. They are aware of the harsh side of life, and it is a good part of their genius that they show us how to face it realistically. Such realism may produce difficulties, but the PSALMS show us, too, how to keep from being overwhelmed by them.

The philosopher and the thinker are not the only ones who frown over the shortness of life. There is hardly a man or woman, alive or dead, who has not had such thoughts. Even the humblest of men has at some time felt a kind of *Why?* and a sadness about how short a time we are permitted on this earth. If you haven't done this yet yourself, then it probably won't be very long now before you will.

We were not here yesterday and we will not be here tomorrow. During the today that we are alive, brief as it is, it would be very nice if there was only sunshine for us, with no gloom. But the script is rarely written for us that way. Here is the way one of the PSALMS puts man's everlasting questions about such matters:

"O Lord, teach me my end,
And what is the extent of my days;
Let me know how I shall end.
Lo, Thou hast fixed my days but as hand-breadths,
And my lifetime is as nothing before Thee;
As a mere breath every man stands. *Selah*
As but a shadow a man walks;
As but a breath he bestirs himself;
He heaps up and knows not who will gather it in.

"And now for what do I wait, O Lord?
My hope is in Thee!
From all my transgressions deliver me!"   *39:5-9*

"With rebukes for guilt Thou dost chastise a man,
And Thou dost wipe out his desire like a cobweb.
Verily, all men are but a breath. *Selah*

"Hear my prayer, O Lord,
And give heed to my cry!
Be not unresponsive to my tears;
For I am a guest with Thee,
A sojourner, like all my ancestors.
Turn Thy gaze away from me, that I may be glad,
Before I go away and be no more."   *39:12-14*

A fat portion of the heavyweight reflections of professional philoso-
phers is implied in this simple poem. "I am a guest" here on earth,
"a sojourner" like all those who have gone before, says the Psalmist.
There must be some reason behind all this, but what is it? It is
all right to speculate on the available evidence, the comings and
goings, the feeling good at times and the feeling bad at others. But
all this is much too mysterious, too brain-defying for any man to
comprehend fully. A trust in something beyond ourselves and what
we see, a faith we find deep within ourselves—that alone can give
meaning to this strange mixture we call life. The Psalmist can face
life with all its contrariness because he trusts that, behind it all,
stands God.

It is typical of Jewish teaching that it is concerned with how one
lives one's life and not just what one believes. Even when thinking

about death, the question becomes: But what does that tell us about how to live?

> "Hear this, all you peoples;
> Give heed, all you dwellers in the world,
> Sons of men, and all mankind,
> Both rich and poor."

49:2-3

> "Even wise men die,
> The fool and the brutish alike perish,
> And leave their wealth to others.
> Their graves are their everlasting home,
> Their dwelling throughout the ages,
> Though lands are named after them."

49:11-12

> "This is the fate of those who are self-sufficient,
> And the end of those who are satisfied with their own words.
>   *Selah*"

49:14

> ". . . Fear not when a man gets rich,
> When the splendor of his house increases;
> For he will take nothing with him when he dies;
> His splendor will not go down after him.
> Though he counts himself happy in being alive,
> And congratulates himself that things go well with him,
> He must join the generation of his fathers;
> Never more will he see the light.
> Man is an ox without understanding,
> He is like the beasts that perish."

49:17-21

This is the ancient statement of that modern maxim, "you can't take it with you." We are being reminded of the smallness of every man. He is just a minnow in the vast Pacific of space and time. Of whom are you jealous? The richest, the most powerful, and even the wisest are all alike, no better than some dumb brute of the field. Wait a bit, and they die. And once dead, there is no such thing as asking who is better off. Why envy anyone for temporary accomplishments?

The same message is found in a Psalm attributed to Moses and widely used at funeral services:

"We come to an end; our years are like a cobweb wiped away.
The length of our life is seventy years,
Perchance through strength eighty years;
But their whole extent is travail and trouble;
For it is quickly cut off and we fly away.
Who knows the power of Thine anger?
Or Thy wrath according to the fear due Thee?
So teach us to number our days
That we may obtain a heart of wisdom.

"Return, O Lord; how long?
And have compassion upon Thy servants.
Satisfy us in the morning with Thy kindness,
That we may shout with joy and be glad throughout our days.
Gladden us in proportion to the days wherein Thou hast
    afflicted us . . .
May Thy work appear unto Thy servants,
And Thy splendor be upon their children.
May the favor of the Lord our God be upon us,
And the work of our hands do Thou establish upon us;
Yea, the work of our hands establish Thou it."   *90:9-17*

Death must come, but we hope that fact will enable us to live our
lives with a "heart of wisdom."

When we do not live wisely

We know we ought to do good with the years God has given us
and we feel great guilt when we have behaved badly. We may try
to hide our sin from people, but what shall we say to God?

"O Lord, Thou hast searched me, and known me.
Thou knowest my downsitting and mine uprising,
Thou understandest my thought afar off.
Thou measurest my going about and my lying down,
And art acquainted with all my ways.
For there is not a word in my tongue,
But, lo, O Lord, Thou knowest it altogether.

"Thou hast hemmed me in behind and before,
And laid Thy hand upon me.

Such knowledge is too wonderful for me;
Too high, I cannot attain unto it.

139:1-8
"Whither shall I go from Thy spirit?
Or whither shall I flee from Thy presence?"

«If I ascend up into heaven, Thou art there;
If I make my bed in the netherworld, behold, Thou art there.
If I take the wings of the morning,
And dwell in the uttermost parts of the sea;
Even there would Thy hand lead me,
139:8-10
And Thy right hand would hold me.»

«Search me, O God, and know my heart,
Try me, and know my thoughts;
And see if there be any way in me that is grievous,
139:23-24
And lead me in the way everlasting.»

It does not take a course in astronomy to make any man aware of his smallness and insignificance in the face of the universe and eternity. Here the poet makes us really feel the wonder and awe in that smallness. He is working out his days in the palm, as it were, of the Lord, conscious of the presence of God and of his own guilt. But in Judaism this does not lead to despair or moral paralysis.

"Out of the depths I cry to Thee, O Lord!
130:1-2
O Lord, hear my voice!"

"If Thou, O Lord, shouldst record iniquities,
O Lord, who could stand?
But with Thee there is forgiveness,
130:3-4
That Thou mayest be revered."

"Hope, O Israel, in the Lord,
For with the Lord is mercy,
And with Him is plenteous redemption.
For He will redeem Israel
130:7-8
From all its guilt."

In another Psalm, the TORAH is compared to the sun. But having been given such godly instruction for his life, it is man's responsibility to live up to it.

"The heavens declare the glory of God,
And the firmament showeth His handiwork;
Day unto day pours forth speech,
And night unto night declares knowledge."   *19:2-3*

"In them hath He set a tent for the sun,
Who is like a bridegroom coming forth from his chamber . . .
And nothing is hid from the heat thereof.

"The law of the Lord is perfect, renewing life;
The decree of the Lord is trustworthy, making wise the simple;
The precepts of the Lord are right, rejoicing the heart;
The command of the Lord is pure, enlightening the eyes . . .
In keeping them there is great reward.

The height of Masada

Who can discern his errors?
Of unconscious ones, hold me guiltless!
Moreover, restrain Thy servant from willful ones,
May they not rule over me! . . .
May the words of my mouth and the meditation of my heart
Be acceptable before Thee,
O Lord, my Rock and my Redeemer!"   *19:5-15*

There is a reason why sin does not become oppressive, why
Judaism is against being gloomy and morbid. Just as God provides
guidance, expecting us to do the right, so, when we try and fail, or
are ready to try again to do what is right, He will forgive us.

«He has not treated us according to our sins,
Nor rewarded us according to our iniquities.
But high as the heavens are above the earth,
So great is His kindness toward them that revere Him.»   *103:10-11*

"Far as the east is from the west,
So far has He removed our offenses from us.
As a father is kind to his children,
So the Lord is kind to those who revere Him.
For He knows our frame;
He remembers that we are but dust.
A man's days are like the grass;
Like a flower of the field, so he blossoms;
For the wind passes over it, and it is not,

And its place knows it no more.
But the kindness of the Lord is from age to age upon those
who revere Him,
And His righteousness to children's children,
For those who keep His covenant,

103:12-18
And remember to observe His precepts."

Psalms of protest and lament

The man who gives his life to attaining justice and mercy for all soon discovers a disturbing fact. Most men aren't interested. They may pretend to care, but when something important to them is involved they swerve from the path, and are likely to do terrible things. And if you don't go along with them, they may even do terrible things to you. In Psalm after Psalm we get a listing of social sins that is remarkably contemporary. People seem to have changed little in 2,500 years.

In this Psalm we hear what seems almost like a modern petition of grievance, presented by a group of victims to City Hall. But here the petition is presented to God:

"Why dost Thou stand afar off, O Lord,
And hide Thyself in times of need?
The wicked in his arrogance consumes the poor;
May they be caught in the schemes which they have devised!

"The wicked sings the praises of his own desires,
And the robber curses, and rejects God;
The wicked in the pride of his countenance does not seek Him;
All his thought is, 'There is no God.'
His ways prosper at all times.
Thy judgments are on high, out of his sight . . .
His mouth is filled with curses and deceit and violence;
Mischief and wrong are under his tongue.
He sits in the lurking-places of villages;
In hiding-places he murders the innocent;
His eyes lie in wait for the unfortunate.
He lurks in secret like a lion in a thicket;
He lurks that he may rob the weak;
He robs the weak when he draws him into his net.
And he bends over, he crouches;

And the unfortunate fall by his mighty men.
He says to himself, 'God has forgotten;
He has hidden His face; He will never see it.' "   *10:1-11*

"The unfortunate leaves himself to Thee;
Thou hast been a helper to the orphan.
Break the arm of the wicked and the evildoer."   *10:14-15*

"Thou hast heard the desire of the meek, O Lord,
Thou dost set Thy mind, Thou dost pay close heed,
So as to do justice to the orphan and the oppressed,
That man who is of the earth may never again strike terror."   *10:17-18*

Notice that last line. It contains the key not only to this Psalm but to thousands of years of human complaint. It cries out against the man who sits on the backs of those beneath him in the scale of money and power. The one causing all the anguish down below is a man "who is of the earth," and he strikes "terror."

In the course of any week each of us is likely to meet or hear about such a person. He seems to care only about power. He may want it to get money, or popularity, or to be able to give away favors. But he wishes primarily to tell other people what they have to do—mostly for him. Such people have been poisoning the mainstream of history since time began. Whether we call them bullies, big shots, crooks, manipulators, or gangsters, each of us will run into his share of them in his life. This particular Psalm is a cry to God for help against those who exploit others for profit. In most civilized countries, such cries bring laws which try to protect the weaker many from the powerful few. But any law is like a net. The cunning fish may elude it, and the powerful one may break holes in it. No manmade law has yet worked perfectly.

Here is another kind of plea, one which Jesus quoted when he was on the cross:

"My God, my God, why hast Thou forsaken me?
And why art Thou far from helping me, at the words of my
    wailing?
My God, I cry by day, but Thou dost not answer;
And by night, and get no rest. . . .
In Thee our fathers trusted;
They trusted and Thou didst deliver them. . . .

But I am a worm and not a man,
A shame to mankind, and despised of the people.
All who see me make sport of me;
22:2-8   They make mouths at me and toss their heads."

Stone mortar and pestle

"Do not stay far from me;
For trouble is near;
For there is none to help. . . .
I am poured out like water,
And all my bones are disjointed.
My heart is like wax,
Melted in the midst of my bosom.
My strength is dried up like a potsherd,
And my tongue cleaves to my palate;
And they lay me in the dust of death.
For dogs have surrounded me.
22:12-17   My hands and my feet are crippled."

In this Psalm we do not hear the despair of someone who laments his condition as a Jew, a member of a nation battered by history. This is rather the outcry of an ordinary man who sees himself as a lone being, so small as to be almost beyond the notice of God. He is "not a man" but a "worm," the lowest of the low. Afflicted in every possible way, he ticks off for us the many symptoms of the devastation he feels. Some of these are likely to seem familiar to most people. There are times for each of us when we feel the full measure of our own smallness.

At such a time, more than at any other, most of us will search for something in which we can invest our hope. Now, all is darkness. . . . But in the next moments, if we could only believe in something, the darkness would pass. The problem is that in the most deeply serious moments we cannot trust only in ourselves, or other people, or the hope that times will get better. We trust in God. His ways are not always understandable but He will not betray us in the end. That is why, in the midst of his agony, the Psalmist complains to God. Here is another example:

"As the hart panteth after the water brooks,
So panteth my soul after Thee, O God. . . .
My tears have been my food day and night,
42:2-4   While they say unto me all the day: 'Where is thy God?'"

"O my God, my soul is cast down within me;
  Therefore do I remember Thee from the land of Jordan . . .
  Deep calleth unto deep at the voice of Thy cataracts;
  All Thy waves and Thy billows are gone over me. . . .
  I will say unto God my Rock: 'Why hast Thou forgotten
    me? . . .'
  Why art thou cast down, O my soul?
  And why moanest thou within me?
  Hope thou in God; for I shall yet praise Him,
  The salvation of my countenance, and my God."   *42:7-12*

The sense of personal woe in this Psalm is all but complete. The
speaker is ground down by his troubles. But more than that, he is
being mocked for the one thing he believes in that makes all his
suffering endurable: "Where is thy God?"

Belief gives one strength in adversity, so the important thing is
to hold firm. When that basic faith goes, the rest of our strength
usually goes with it.

We might ask, What if the belief is false—not only a lie, but a
vicious lie? After all, didn't the average Nazi believe totally in
Adolph Hitler? Such things are of course possible. They happen to
people more often than they probably should. Because there is
something in each of us that makes us *want* to find something,
anything, in which to believe. Here the Jewish tradition coupled
with modern intelligence is very helpful. A good man will ask
not only, What do I gain by this belief?, but, Who is hurt by this
belief? What has been the experience of Judaism in such matters
and what has been the experience of mankind? Anyone might be
wrong about his decision, but thinking about it in this way should
make him much more aware of what he is choosing.

Our people, too, have suffered

The Jewish people, bounced around by history, have usually been
forced to live out their lives in what a Chinese curse has called
"interesting times." Here, in one of the Psalms, they are reacting
to an especially painful disaster: the destruction of the Temple.

". . . The enemy has destroyed everything in the Temple.
  Thy foes roar in the midst of Thine assembly;
  They set up their own signs as signs. . . .
  They have set Thy sanctuary on fire;

They have defiled to the ground the dwelling-place of Thy
     name.
They said to themselves, 'We will oppress them also.'
They burned all the meeting-places of God in the land. . . .
How long, O God, shall the foe blaspheme?

74:3-10

Shall the enemy revile Thy name forever?"

"Do not give the life of Thy turtledove to the wild beasts;
Do not forget the life of Thine afflicted ones forever.
Have regard to the Covenant;
For the dark places of the land are full of the
     habitations of violence . . .

74:19-22

Arise, O God, plead Thine own cause . . ."

Another great lament, written on the same theme, indicates the
problem of trying to fix the historical background of a poem. Is
this about the Babylonian destruction, or is it about Antiochus, 400
years later, who defiled but did not destroy the Temple? Whichever
is true, the words describe many a Jewish experience of anguish and
desertion. And the call to God to act was put in the traditional
Passover Haggadah, to be said when the door was opened for Elijah.
He was to announce the coming of the Messiah, and these lines
were a call for the Day of Judgment and a vindication of Israel.

"O God . . .
They have defiled Thy Holy Temple;
They have laid Jerusalem in ruins.
They have given the corpses of Thy servants
As food to the birds of the air. . . .
We are become a taunt for our neighbors,
Derision and mockery for those around us.

"How long, O Lord, wilt Thou be angry forever?
Will Thy jealousy burn like fire?
Pour out Thy wrath upon the nations who do not acknowledge
     Thee,
And upon the kingdoms that do not invoke Thy name;
For they have destroyed Jacob,
And have laid waste his habitation.
Do not remember against us our early sins;

May Thy mercies quickly meet us,
For we are brought very low.

"Help us, O saving God,
  Because of the glory of Thy name;
  Deliver us and forgive our sins for Thy name's sake. . . ." 79:1-9
The picture of a gardener caring for a vine is often used in the
Bible to describe the relation between God and the Jews. (Husband
and wife, and partners in a contract, are two other great similes.)
Here it is used to bring home the difficulty in understanding why
God does not protect His people:

Cedar of Lebanon

"Thou didst remove a vine from Egypt;
  Thou didst expel the nations and replant it;
  Thou didst smooth the way for it,
  So that it struck root and filled the land.
  The mountains were covered with its shade,
  And the cedars of God with its branches.
  It sent forth its boughs to the sea,
  And its tendrils to the river.
  Why, then, hast Thou broken down its walls,
  So that all who pass by pluck its fruit?
  The wild boar devours it,
  And the beasts of the field feed upon it." 80:9-14

"O God of hosts, restore us;
  And let Thy face shine that we may be delivered." 80:20
If God has chosen this particular people for His own, and if they
believe in Him, then why have they been permitted to suffer? That
is the community's version of Job's problem. It finds frequent expression in the PSALMS. Being in Covenant with God does not mean
immunity to misfortune. The Jews are chosen for service, not luxury
or privilege. As the constant reminder to mankind of God and His
demands, the Jews have drawn the resentment and resistance of
that same mankind. And God, not interfering with the freedom He
has given to men, has let Israel be badly battered—but not destroyed!
What Israel has, on a human level, is confidence that its cause
is right. The man who believes intensely in *something* is bound to
have a greater emotional and even practical momentum over the

road of life than the one who believes in nothing. And one other thing: Should calamity come, the man who believes is more likely to survive than is the man who does not believe. It has been the intensity of Jewish belief in God, and the conviction that the Jews were truly serving Him, which, more than any other human factor, has kept our people on their feet, marching through history for four thousand years.

Everyone has known, at some time in his life, the pangs of homesickness, the sense of melancholy that comes from being in a faraway place that is not one's own. This deep longing for one's own place, one's homeland, has often been felt by communities, particularly one as old and as long dispersed as the Jewish people. Already in Biblical days, during the Babylonian Exile, this mood of longing was expressed with unparalleled power and feeling:

"By the rivers of Babylon,
There we sat down, and wept,
When we remembered Zion.
Upon the poplars, in the midst of her,
We hung our harps.
For there our captors
Demanded of us songs,
And our tormentors, mirth:
'Sing us some of the songs of Zion.'

"How could we sing the song of the Lord
In a foreign land?
If I forget you, O Jerusalem,
May my right hand fail me!
May my tongue cleave to my palate,
If I do not remember you;
If I set not Jerusalem
137:1-6   Above my highest joy!"

Next time you see an American Negro wearing African dress or hairdo, think of this Psalm. The person you are looking at is probably expressing in his own way a similar feeling.

Psalms of trust

Few of us feel strong enough to take on the entire world all by ourselves. Even as a part of the Jewish people, to wait and work

Boat towed along Tigris

for the days of the Messiah is often more burdensome than we can bear. Yet this is the kind of challenge God has given us. The Psalmists not only know how difficult life can be, but they tell us how they are able to stand it. They have a deep and abiding faith in God. That does not mean they know all the answers or have no troubles. As we have seen, they are realists and suffer greatly, often from God's slowness in acting or in saving them. Yet, like Job, they are not atheists. They believe even though they are deeply disturbed and in pain. Walt Whitman called faith "the antiseptic of the soul." It is the great healer. Many of the PSALMS are filled with the sense of serenity that comes, even in the midst of trouble, to those who have put their faith in God.

"How many are my foes, O Lord!
  Many rise up against me.
  Many say concerning me:
'There is no help for him in God.' *Selah*

"But Thou, O Lord, art a shield about me,
  My glory, and the one who raises my head.
  I cry aloud to the Lord,
  And He answers me from His holy hill. *Selah*

"I lie down and sleep;
  I awake, for the Lord sustains me.
  I am not afraid of the myriads of people
  That have beset me round about. . . ."   3:2-7

These lines tell of the strength that comes from faith. Once you have a sense of purpose, a sense of the rightness of what you are about—we call it "commitment"—then you are less likely to be turned aside. Think of the Prophets, then think of the Jews in history. Most people you know seem to disagree with you? It will not matter. Some are even raising their hands against you? This will not matter, either. The man who feels that there is right and justice about what he is doing is bound to feel his own strength. It is this belief that makes him feel almost mystically protected against the harsh ideas—and sometimes even the actions—of those who do not agree with him.

It is easy to point out that this kind of commitment can be felt equally by the Nazi, the religious fanatic, and the mental case.

Golden cup

That is true, and deciding on what is ultimately right is not easy. It is, even for the wisest of men, a lifelong matter. And that is what your religion is about. It will, all your life, challenge your deeds and sensitize your conscience. It will bring to your help the ideas—and the experience—not merely of one man in one time and one place, but of the Jewish community as a whole. The responsibility for the way you lead your life is still yours. Choosing a system of values to which you are committed is part of the bill for being *human* beings. The amount of time any of us will live on this planet is very short, even at best. It is important to make sure not only that we have those values, but that they are of the kind that are worth our sticking out our necks. Judaism is our best single aid in living up to the responsibilities of deciding who we are and who we want to be.

On the subject of trust, this is the world's greatest poem, perhaps because it is as simple as its theme is sublime:

יְיָ רֹעִי לֹא אֶחְסָר:

בִּנְאוֹת דֶּשֶׁא יַרְבִּיצֵנִי. עַל־מֵי מְנֻחוֹת יְנַהֲלֵנִי:

נַפְשִׁי יְשׁוֹבֵב. יַנְחֵנִי בְמַעְגְּלֵי־צֶדֶק לְמַעַן שְׁמוֹ:

גַּם כִּי־אֵלֵךְ בְּגֵיא צַלְמָוֶת לֹא־אִירָא רָע. כִּי־אַתָּה עִמָּדִי.

שִׁבְטְךָ וּמִשְׁעַנְתֶּךָ הֵמָּה יְנַחֲמֻנִי:

תַּעֲרֹךְ לְפָנַי שֻׁלְחָן נֶגֶד צֹרְרָי. דִּשַּׁנְתָּ בַשֶּׁמֶן רֹאשִׁי כּוֹסִי רְוָיָה:

אַךְ טוֹב וָחֶסֶד יִרְדְּפוּנִי כָּל־יְמֵי חַיָּי.

וְשַׁבְתִּי בְּבֵית יְיָ לְאֹרֶךְ יָמִים:

«The Lord is my shepherd; I shall not want.
  He maketh me to lie down in green pastures;
  He leadeth me beside the still waters.
  He restoreth my soul;
  He guideth me in straight paths for His name's sake.
  Yea, though I walk through the valley of the shadow of death,
  I will fear no evil,
  For Thou art with me;
  Thy rod and Thy staff,
  They comfort me.
  Thou preparest a table before me in the presence of mine
    enemies;
  Thou hast anointed my head with oil; my cup runneth over.

Surely goodness and mercy shall follow me all the days of
　　my life;
And I shall dwell in the House of the Lord for ever.»　　　*Psalm 23*

This Psalm has given comfort to men and women in the farthest
corners of the world for many centuries. It was written by Jews,
for Jews, but its profound and persuasive words have leaped over
the walls of our religion and made it, in a way, the property of all
men who believe in God.

　Here are two other great expressions of confidence in God. First:
"The Lord is my Light and my Salvation; whom shall I fear?
　The Lord is the refuge of my life; of whom shall I be afraid? . . .
　Though a host encamp against me, my heart will not fear;
　Though war arise against me, in this will I be confident.

"One thing I ask from the Lord, that do I seek;
　That I may dwell in the House of the Lord all the days of
　　my life . . .
　For He will hide me in His pavilion, on the day of trouble;
　He will conceal me in His secret tent,
　He will set me up upon a rock.
　And now my head is high above my foes on every side;
　And I will sacrifice in His tent sacrifices with shouts;
　I will sing and make music to the Lord. . . ."　　　*27:1-6*

　The other is one of a series in which each poem is called "A Song
of Ascents." Scholars have puzzled for years over the meaning of
that term "ascents." Is it the steps between the courts of the Temple
on which the Levites sang Psalms during the sacrificial services? Is
it the pilgrimage to Jerusalem, made three times a year, during
which one must ascend the mountains? Is it some inner word-play
in the poems, moving from verse to verse? We do not know. But
there is no question as to the beauty of these poems. Note the
simplicity and effectiveness of this one:
«I will lift up mine eyes unto the mountains:
　From whence shall my help come?
　My help cometh from the Lord,
　Who made heaven and earth.

«He will not suffer thy foot to be moved;
　He that keepeth thee will not slumber.

Behold, He that keepeth Israel
Doth neither slumber nor sleep.

«The Lord is thy keeper;
The Lord is thy shade upon thy right hand.
The sun shall not smite thee by day,
Nor the moon by night.

«The Lord shall keep thee from all evil;
He shall keep thy soul.

«The Lord shall guard thy going out and thy coming in,
Psalm 121   From this time forth and for ever.»

Psalms of triumph and rejoicing

Man's condition on earth has never been an easy one. If he isn't beset by bad leaders or bad weather, then it's bad crops or bad business conditions, bad friends, bad debts, or even bad mates.

Moments of great reward and fulfillment are the exception rather than the rule. Perhaps if they happened too frequently we would not cherish them so much. Human nature is like that. But life is not all pain and suffering. There are times when long, hard work, when faithfulness, when persistence despite everything, result in accomplishment. For the individual, that may be recovery from an accident, the buying of a home, winning a degree, rearing a difficult child to responsible adulthood. But there are such moments for communities as well. When the State of Israel was established, or when the United States passed its first meaningful national civil rights law, masses of men knew something great had happened in their lives.

The Jewish people come especially alive in the memory of such moments—at Mt. Sinai, Mt. Carmel, and in the Temple at Jerusalem—and in the hope of another such moment, the days of the Messiah. Judaism is basically an optimistic faith even though it is also centered on realism. It does not want a faith built on hiding from things or based on seeing only the good. That would soon die.

A reminder. These special quotation marks « » denote passages to be learned by heart.

But because of his faith in God, the Jew can face all the ugliness of the world and not be overwhelmed by it. Faith in God and His ultimate help for man turns realism into optimism. So there is not just a Jewish sense of serene trust and confidence in God but one of triumph and rejoicing when His power has been made evident. In the everyday affairs of our lives, we simply bless Him with the *Shehecheyanu* blessing. In the greater experiences we repeat today ancient words of exultation:

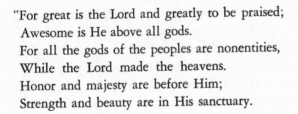

"Sing to the Lord a new song;
Sing to the Lord, all the earth;
Sing to the Lord, bless His name;
Publish His deliverance abroad from day to day.
Tell among the nations His glory,
Among all the peoples, His wonders.

Head from ancient Persia

"For great is the Lord and greatly to be praised;
Awesome is He above all gods.
For all the gods of the peoples are nonentities,
While the Lord made the heavens.
Honor and majesty are before Him;
Strength and beauty are in His sanctuary.

"Ascribe to the Lord, O families of peoples,
Ascribe to the Lord glory and strength.
Ascribe to the Lord the glory of His name;
Bring an offering and come into His courts.
Worship the Lord in holy array;
Tremble before Him, all the earth."

96:1-9

One group of Psalms uses, as a refrain, the word *Hallelujah*. Note the odd spelling of this word, with the German "j" instead of a "y" as in all Biblical words rendered into English, *e.g.,* Elijah. It means "praise the Lord," and is one of the few Hebrew words carried over directly into English. *Amen,* which means "so be it," and *Selah,* the meaning of which is unknown, are two others.

All of the Hallelujah Psalms deal with the praise of God for His great help. Some of these Psalms (113-118) are said on special festivals, and are known as the *Hallel,* which is short for Hallelujah. In Psalm 113 the thanksgiving would appear to be for His help to individuals:

"Hallelujah!
Praise, O servants of the Lord,
Praise the name of the Lord!
Blessed be the name of the Lord,
From henceforth even for ever.
From the rising of the sun unto its setting,
Let the Lord's name be praised.

"High above all heavens is the Lord,
Above the heavens is His glory.
Who is like the Lord, our God,
Seated on high, Seeing far below,
In the heavens and on the earth?

Egyptian sea-trade ship

"He lifts up the poor from the dust;
He raises the needy from the refuse heap,
To make them sit with princes,
With the princes of His people.
He makes the childless woman abide in the household
As the happy mother of its children.

Psalm 113   Hallelujah!"

Psalm 118 speaks in the first person, "I," so it seems quite individual. But there are so many references to groups that it is obviously also meant to apply to the community. That might seem a strange mixture to us, but in ancient times the single person did not feel as isolated from his folk as we do. His own person and his people sort of merged into each other. Often in the PSALMS, when the speaker says "I," one cannot be sure whether it is the people of Israel or only one Jew who is meant.

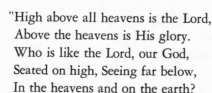

הוֹדוּ לַיָי כִּי־טוֹב. כִּי לְעוֹלָם חַסְדּוֹ:

יֹאמַר־נָא יִשְׂרָאֵל. כִּי לְעוֹלָם חַסְדּוֹ:

יֹאמְרוּ־נָא בֵית־אַהֲרֹן, כִּי לְעוֹלָם חַסְדּוֹ:

יֹאמְרוּ־נָא יִרְאֵי יְיָ. כִּי לְעוֹלָם חַסְדּוֹ:

"Give thanks to the Lord; For He is good,
For His kindness is everlasting.
Let Israel now say,
That His kindness is everlasting.

Let the house of Aaron now say,
That His kindness is everlasting.
Let those that revere the Lord now say,
That His kindness is everlasting.

"When in straits, I called upon the Lord;
He answered me with abundant room.
With the Lord for me, I do not fear
What man may do to me.
With the Lord for me as my helper,
I shall gaze in triumph on those who hate me.
It is better to seek refuge in the Lord
Than to trust in man.
It is better to seek refuge in the Lord
Than to trust in princes.
Though all nations surround me,
In the name of the Lord I will ward them off."

118:1-10

And,

לֹא־אָמוּת כִּי־אֶחְיֶה. וַאֲסַפֵּר מַעֲשֵׂי יָהּ:

יַסֹּר יִסְּרַנִּי יָּהּ. וְלַמָּוֶת לֹא נְתָנָנִי:

פִּתְחוּ־לִי שַׁעֲרֵי־צֶדֶק. אָבֹא־בָם אוֹדֶה יָהּ.

זֶה־הַשַּׁעַר לַיְיָ. צַדִּיקִים יָבֹאוּ בוֹ:

אוֹדְךָ כִּי עֲנִיתָנִי. וַתְּהִי־לִי לִישׁוּעָה:

אֶבֶן מָאֲסוּ הַבּוֹנִים. הָיְתָה לְרֹאשׁ פִּנָּה:

מֵאֵת יְיָ הָיְתָה זֹּאת. הִיא נִפְלָאת בְּעֵינֵינוּ:

זֶה־הַיּוֹם עָשָׂה יְיָ. נָגִילָה וְנִשְׂמְחָה בוֹ:

"I shall not die, but live
To tell the deeds of the Lord.
The Lord has disciplined me severely;
But He has not given me up to death.
Open for me the gates of righteousness,
That I may enter through them to give thanks to the Lord.
This is the gate of the Lord,
Through which the righteous may enter.
I thank Thee that Thou hast answered me,
And hast become my Deliverance.

"The stone that the builders rejected
Has become the chief cornerstone.

"From the Lord has this come,
It is wonderful in our eyes.
This is the day that the Lord has made;

118:17-24   Let us rejoice and be glad therein!"

It is easy to understand why the Hallel is recited as part of the morning service during the three joyous festivals, Pesach, Shavuot, and Sukkot. Indeed, the BOOK OF PSALMS closes on a similar note of triumph and rejoicing. It seems more a list than a poem, but if you have ever heard it sung—Lewandowski's arrangement has been widely used by choirs—you will have a better idea of what it seeks to convey:

"Hallelujah!
Praise God in His sanctuary!
Praise Him in His mighty firmament!
Praise Him for His mighty deeds!
Praise Him for His abundant greatness!
Praise Him with the blast of the horn!
Praise Him with lyre and lute!
Praise Him with drum and dance!
Praise Him with strings and pipe!
Praise Him with clanging cymbals!
Praise Him with crashing cymbals!
Let everything that breathes praise the Lord!

Psalm 150   Hallelujah!"

Some prose about these poems

We do not know who wrote the PSALMS. If we were to believe what we read in many of the titles, we would assume that some of the greatest names in early Jewish history took part in the writing. Moses, David, and Solomon are among them. We know that David was a man of great poetic gifts, because there are evidences of this in other parts of the Bible. So too, we know that Solomon wrote many songs. It is certainly possible that a number of these poems were written by the men to whom they are credited. It is even more likely that most of the PSALMS were the work of unknown poets who set them down to express their deepest feelings.

Very probably they were transmitted from generation to generation by word of mouth, like the poems of Homer or the Norse sagas. They are a great epic of feeling that grew gradually, over the years. Many were undoubtedly written to accompany the service in the Temple, and so were preserved and transmitted by the Levites. In time, they were put together and incorporated into the Bible as the supreme collection of religious poetry.

Of all the books of the Bible, this is the one which tells us most about the capacity of the human spirit to hang on, to endure, when it has faith in God. In the blackest periods of despair, whether in war, famine, or more intensely personal disaster, those with some private rock to cling to feel most surely that they will survive the ordeal—and experience has proved that these are the ones who, in most cases, *do* survive.

Silver spoon

In this collection of poems, it is possible to find words to represent every level of human experience, from the deepest sorrow and despair up to the outer extreme of joy. Most of the intermediate stations of human feeling are represented here, too. There are disappointment and repentance, the sense of life and the sense of death, love and sin, comfort and unease, exaltation and condemnation. It is a great catalogue of the full range of human feeling.

No other book of the Bible has been made so completely a part of the standard spiritual equipment of thoughtful men and women everywhere. The PSALMS have become the common currency of a large portion of mankind. They deal with the most profound of human experiences, the condition of the soul as it navigates through the storms and calms of life. And because of the beauty and power with which they do this, they grow on one as the years go by.

When you are young, and life has touched you so far only with the tips of its fingers, the full meaning of these poems may slip past you. A reading of them may cause you to wonder what all the praise is about. These poems do not have the immediate appeal of tales of battle and intrigue, or the cries of some Prophet who is denouncing colorful sin. They call out to something that lies deep inside the reader.

It is only after you have grown a bit older that you realize, along the way, how much more meaning there seems to be now than when you first came across the PSALMS in your youth. Perhaps that is their greatest praise, that you can live with them all your life.

CONCLUSION

A FEW WORDS IN PARTING

CHAPTER 13

WE HAVE COME to the end of our brief tour through the last part of the Bible. What can we say now about a book that has meant so much, for so long, to so many people?

In some respects, the Bible may be compared with the sun. It was here long before you and I arrived and it will remain here long after we leave. It is a visible presence in our lives, continually reminding us of things that are eternal. And when there are no clouds, it provides us with needed warmth and hope, a sense of health and lightness of spirit. When you try to imagine a world without the sun, you see there could be no spring, whether in nature or in our hearts.

A physicist may list for us the many diverse elements of which the sun is composed. Things like carbon and gases, none of which have a very romantic sound. It does not matter. It is the *effect* of the sun on us that is important. In the same way, a man of science may point out that the Bible contains obvious errors, contradictions, and other elements that keep it from being an exact document. This again does not matter, because like the sun the Bible has been a source of lasting good over many centuries. It gives light and it gives warmth, despite its occasional lapses from what we would call "the facts." It does not have the painstaking accuracy of your local telephone directory, but remember that your phone book must have its facts checked every year. The Bible has remained unchanged for thousands of years, and the message it has to offer is far more full of meaning than anything ever announced over a telephone.

There is one part of the Bible's message that is especially important—the need for man to believe in God. Each of us must believe, with the fullest kind of commitment, that something very important to us happens to be true. Otherwise, we and our lives become empty and meaningless.

In the year 131 C.E., the Roman Emperor Hadrian thought he had the perfect way to solve his problems with those troublesome people in Judea. He would cause all Jewish beliefs to disappear. Appropriate laws were soon laid down. It was forbidden to observe the Sabbath or any other holy day. There could be no performance of any Hebrew ritual in public. Circumcision was made illegal. Public instruction in the laws of Moses became taboo under pain of death. Especially severe taxes were put upon the Jews. And to make sure that the lesson was driven home, pagan temples were erected by the Romans all over Jerusalem.

Resentment exploded into armed rebellion. For three years they fought back in the devastating Bar Kochba revolt. The land was drenched with blood, but the Roman power was too strong. Over a million Jews died by violence or starvation in the struggle against this early Hitler. They lost the war. And yet what was the result?

In time it was the Roman Empire that disappeared. The Jews were able to survive this enemy, just as they had survived so many before, and as they have survived so many others since. The more their faith was put under attack, the more dear and true it became to them. Their powers of survival were directly related to their capacity for hope. And throughout history, the hopes of the Jews have rested firmly on their belief in their God.

Ur ziggurat

There is good reason to assume that the Jews would have disappeared into the rubbish heap of history long ago, if not for their belief in God. They would now be a mere footnote, at best a few paragraphs, like the Dacians, the Scythians, or the worshippers of Mithra. In a way, the best proof for the reality of God is the continued existence of the Children of Israel. But, forgetting the Jews for a moment, think of all that has been produced in this world by men who were directly motivated by a strong feeling about God. Renaissance art, Greek drama, and miles of poetry are only one part of it. Even science owes a great debt to this all-encompassing belief. Because of the curiosity that stimulated alchemists, court magicians, and such inquiring spirits, we made many early advances in astronomy, medicine, and other sciences. And above all, in moral justice and the law.

Assume, for the sake of argument, that you have come to the Bible with no preconceived ideas about God or religion. Assume further that you have just read the WISDOM WRITINGS. Now ask yourself a question: Has this anything to say to me? Only a fool would answer No. It is one of the world's great source books of wisdom and guidance for the conduct of one's life. It understands people and their relations with each other. Moreover, it understands that men are truly human, with one another or as a society, only when they have a sense of that transcendent reality we call God, and when they try to apply that insight to every aspect of their existence. The men who wrote the books of the Bible had an unparalleled sensitivity to God, and, therefore, to what it means to be truly a man. They certainly did not know everything, but time, history, and human experience have proved that they knew the most important things. They have tried to teach these things to anyone who cares to learn. And they have expressed their lessons in a language and form that have never been surpassed.

Man is an "inquiring animal," and because of this, men are bound to disagree on the things they happen to believe in. Argument is the classic Jewish method of study, and our religion gives remarkable freedom to question and to debate what is finally true. Think of JOB and of the PSALMS. If man is to move in the direction of a better life, it is necessary for him to reason. And if he is to feel any zest in the daily round of living, it is necessary for him to believe in something. Judaism has always been a religion which gloried in intellectuality. Think of EZRA and the PROVERBS. But along with this it has also been a religion of passion and heart. Think of RUTH and the SONG OF SONGS.

We come here to the core of the problem. Reason and faith are like two men who must share the driving on a long automobile trip through strange and rough country, in which there is no time to stop. Reason drives mainly in daylight, when the obstacles are often clear. Faith manages the wheel, as a rule, through gloom and darkness, when the road is less clearly marked. Each driver thinks it has the more important job. The truth is that they depend on each other, and both are needed to make the trip successfully. It takes many books to make a Bible, many moods to make a man. No one

Biblical book, or chapter, or verse, gives us the whole truth—but together they make up the finest book of religious teaching mankind has ever known. We need to put heart and head together—each of us—to become a full person. When we are one, whole and integrated, then we shall know Him who is One. And knowing Him we shall have done our part to bring the day on which all men will know Him as One in their lives.